MW00574394

To Exhort
and Reprove

To Exhort
and Reprove

Audience Response to the Chiastic Structures
of Paul's Letter to Titus

Paul S. Jeon

PICKWICK *Publications* · Eugene, Oregon

TO EXHORT AND REPROVE
Audience Response to the Chiastic Structures of Paul's Letter to Titus

Copyright © 2012 Paul S. Jeon. All rights reserved. Except for brief quotations in critical publications or reviews, no part of this book may be reproduced in any manner without prior written permission from the publisher. Write: Permissions, Wipf and Stock Publishers, 199 W. 8th Ave., Suite 3, Eugene, OR 97401.

Pickwick Publications
An Imprint of Wipf and Stock Publishers
199 W. 8th Ave., Suite 3
Eugene, OR 97401

www.wipfandstock.com

ISBN 13: 978–1-61097–505–6

Cataloguing-in-Publication data:

Jeon, Paul S.

To exhort and reprove : audience response to the chiastic structures of Paul's letter to Titus / Paul S. Jeon.

xii + 134 p. ; 23 cm. Includes bibliographical references.

ISBN 13: 978–1-61097–505–6

1. Bible N.T. Titus—Criticism, interpretation, etc. I. Title.

BS2755.3 J35 2012

Manufactured in the U.S.A.

*To my parents
who taught me to live according
to the hope of eternal life*

Contents

Acknowledgments

FIRST, I WANT TO thank John Paul Heil for suggesting the topic and for providing meticulous guidance throughout the entire process of writing my dissertation, which served as the basis for this current study. He is a model of scholarly diligence and excellence. Second, I want to thank Frank J. Matera and Francis T. Gignac for reading my dissertation manuscript carefully and offering constructive criticism. Both have taught me to love New Testament Greek and Paul's letters. I am especially grateful to my family and friends, who provided much joy and encouragement throughout my doctoral work. I also thank NewCity Church for giving me the opportunity to serve as their pastor while completing my PhD. Finally, I thank my wife Geena Jeon, who is my best friend, and my precious son, Christian Jeon, who is my delight.

Abbreviations

AB	Anchor Bible
AGAJU	Arbeiten zur Geschichte des antiken Judentums und des Urchristentums
BDAG	W. Bauer, W. F. Arndt, and F. W. Gingrich (3d ed.; rev. by F. W. Danker), *Greek-English Lexicon of the NT*
BDF	F. Blass, A. Debrunner, and R. W. Funk, *A Greek Grammar of the NT*
Bib	*Biblica*
BSac	*Bibliotheca Sacra*
BTB	*Biblical Theology Bulletin*
BZ	*Biblische Zeitschrift*
CBQ	*Catholic Biblical Quarterly*
CH	*Church History*
CTR	*Criswell Theological Review*
EBib	Études bibliques
EDNT	H. Balz and G. Schneider (eds.), *Exegetical Dictionary of the New Testament*
ESV	*English Standard Version*
FRLANT	Forschungen zur Religion und Literatur des Alten und Neuen Testaments
HBT	*Horizons in Biblical Theology*
ICC	International Critical Commentary
JBL	*Journal of Biblical Literature*
JETS	*Journal of the Evangelical Theological Society*
JSNT	*Journal for the Study of the New Testament*
JSNTSup	JSNT, Supplement Series
JTS	*Journal of Theological Studies*
LSJ	Liddell-Scott-Jones, *Greek-English Lexicon*

MM	J. H. Moulton and G. Milligan, *The Vocabulary of the Greek Testament*
NAB	*New American Bible*
Neot	*Neotestamentica*
NET	*New English Translation*
NIBC	New International Biblical Commentary
NIGTC	New International Greek Testament Commentary
NovT	*Novum Testamentum*
NovTSup	NovT, Supplements
NRSV	*New Revised Standard Version*
NTL	New Testament Library
NTS	*New Testament Studies*
ÖBS	Österreichische biblische Studien
RB	*Revue biblique*
ResQ	*Restoration Quarterly*
RHPR	*Revue d'histoire et de philosophie religieuses*
SBLDS	SBL Dissertation Series
SBT	Studies in Biblical Theology
SNTSMS	Society for New Testament Studies Monograph Series
TCGNT	B. M. Metzger, *A Textual Commentary on the Greek New Testament*
TLNT	C. Spicq and J. D. Ernest, *Theological Lexicon of the New Testament*
TynBul	*Tyndale Bulletin*
TynNTC	Tyndale New Testament Commentaries
WBC	Word Biblical Commentary
WMANT	Wissenschaftliche Monographien zum Alten und Neuen Testament
WUNT	Wissenschaftliche Untersuchungen zum Neuen Testament

1

Introduction

TITUS: EXHORT AND REPROVE TO COMMENDABLE WORKS ACCORDING TO THE HOPE OF ETERNAL LIFE

The words in the heading, "Titus: Exhort and Reprove to Commendable Works according to the Hope of Eternal Life," have been carefully chosen to indicate what I believe is the main theme throughout Paul's letter to Titus.[1] In this book I propose a new chiastic structure of four units that covers and organizes the entire letter. In addition, I show that each of these units exhibits its own chiastic structure. These macro- and micro-chiastic patterns are necessary for understanding what and how Paul, the implied author of the letter to Titus, is communicating to his implied audience.[2]

The words "exhort and reprove" encapsulate the overall tone of Titus as a letter imploring the audience—in particular Titus—to exhort and reprove one another to commendable works. The verb "exhort" (παρακαλέω) occurs three times throughout the letter (1:9; 2:6, 15). The verb "reprove" (ἐλέγχω) also occurs three times (1:9, 13; 2:15). Although the verb "exhort" occurs explicitly in isolation only in 2:6—"Similarly, exhort the younger men to be sensible," the adverb "similarly" clearly indicates that the verb is implied in the multiple exhortations to the other members of the audience (2:1–10). Paul employs the verb "reprove" in isolation in 1:13—"Therefore reprove them severely," referring to the

---

1. I will address the question of authorship in the next section.

2. For similar presentations of the comprehensive chiastic structures present in Philemon, Ephesians, Colossians, and Philippians, see Heil, "The Chiastic Structure and Meaning of Paul's Letter to Philemon," 178–206; idem, *Ephesians: Empowerment to Walk*; idem, *Colossians: Encouragement to Walk*; idem, *Philippians: Let Us Rejoice in Being Conformed to Christ*.

1

"many rebels, empty-talkers and deceivers . . . who are upsetting whole households, teaching what is not necessary" (1:10–11). The two verbs occur together in 1:9 where Paul summarizes the elder's basic duty "to exhort with sound doctrine and reprove those who oppose." They also occur together in 2:15 where Paul commands Titus to "speak and exhort and reprove with all command."

The theme of exhortation and reproof, however, is not limited to sections of the letter with the explicit occurrences of these verbs. Included are other connotations and synonyms of theme throughout the letter. From the outset, Paul relates his apostolic calling to the audience's "recognition of the truth that is according to godliness" (1:1). His apostolic calling is accomplished through the exhortations and reproofs that are communicated through the reading of this letter. In addition, although neither verb occurs in the final chapter of Titus, both are clearly implied. Titus 3:4–7 contains the kind of sound teachings with which the elder is to exhort and reprove. In 3:8 Paul commands that Titus is to "insist" (διαβεβαιοῦσθαι) about these things, which inevitably entails exhortation and reproof. Finally, Titus 3:10–11 indicates that a heretical person is to be reproved and then dismissed if he persists in rebellion after two warnings.

The selection of the phrase "commendable works" as the goal of exhortation and reproof is intended to reflect the letter's emphasis on the appropriate lifestyle that should result from a recognition of the truth, which is summarized as the appearance of God's grace (2:11–14) and the appearance of God's kindness (3:2–7). The first majestic passage concludes with an explicit reference to commendable works—"[Christ] gave himself on behalf of us, so that he might redeem us from all lawlessness and cleanse for himself a special people, zealous for commendable works" (2:14). The second equally majestic passage is also followed by an explicit reference to commendable works: "Faithful is the word, and about these things I want you to insist, so that those who have faith in God may be intent to engage in commendable works" (3:8). While Paul maintains that he and the audience are not saved from works done in righteousness (3:4–5), he makes clear throughout the letter that true faith must be accompanied by good works. Thus, all true believers are to commit themselves to commendable works unlike those who "profess to know God but by their works they deny, being vile and disobedient and unqualified for all good work" (1:16).

The noun "work" (ἔργον) occurs eight times throughout the letter (1:16 [2x]; 2:7, 14; 3:1, 5, 8, 14). Its first two occurrences are found in 1:16, as noted above, where Paul, after comparing the clean with the defiled and unfaithful, condemns the latter for invalidating their faith by their "works" and for being "unqualified for all good work." In 2:7 Paul reminds Titus that in addition to exhorting and reproving, he is to present himself "as a model of commendable works." In 2:14 Paul states that the purpose of Christ's self-sacrifices was to "redeem . . . for himself a special people, zealous for commendable works," which have been described concretely for the audience in 2:1–10. In 3:1 Paul reminds the audience members that they are "to submit to ruling authorities, to be obedient, to be ready for every good work," in obvious contrast to those who are "unqualified for all good work." As noted above, in 3:5 and 3:8 Paul reminds the audience that while salvation is "not from works," it should result in a deep commitment to "commendable works." Finally, in 3:14, the penultimate verse of the letter, Paul writes as a fitting conclusion, "And let our own also learn to engage in commendable works for urgent needs, so that they might not be unfruitful."

Although the noun "work" does not occur for most of Titus 1, Paul's concern for commendable works is no less strong than elsewhere in the letter. In the opening verse of the letter, Paul relates his apostolic calling to the audience's "recognition of the truth that is according to godliness." "Godliness" (εὐσέβεια), which BDAG defines as "awesome respect accorded to God, devoutness, piety," must—as the letter reiterates, especially in 1:16—be expressed through commendable works. In addition, the instructions concerning elders (1:5–9) highlight both their calling to the commendable work of exhorting and reproving according to sound doctrine and their character as men who are already known for their commendable works both inside (1:6) and outside (1:7–8) their homes.

Finally, the choice of the phrase "according to the hope of eternal life" is meant to capture the basis of exhorting and reproving to commendable works. The term "hope" (ἐλπίς) occurs several times in the letter, once in each chapter (1:2; 2:13; 3:7). Paul grounds his own apostolic calling and work of exhortation and reproof "on the basis of the hope of eternal life" (1:2). He then defines eternal life as that which "God, who cannot lie, promised before eternal ages" (1:2). Therefore, the hope of eternal life is a reliable hope.

In 2:13 Paul describes the disposition of believers in terms of "awaiting the blessed hope," which he defines further as "the appearance of the glory of our great God and savior Jesus Christ." At this time, all those who have faith in God will share in the glory of Christ. This verse is preceded by a summary of the ethical life described in terms of "denying ungodliness and worldly desires" and pursuing sensibility, righteousness, and godliness (2:12). It is important to note how Paul grounds the present ethical life not only in the past—"For the grace of God has appeared, saving all human beings" (2:11)—but also in the future hope of eternal life.

Finally, in 3:7 Paul employs the term in his brief summary of the gospel—"so that being made righteous by his grace we might become heirs according to the hope of eternal life." Paul again relates this hope to a commitment "to engage in commendable works" (3:8). As recipients of the hope of eternal life, the audience are to be ready to carry out all good work. In summary, then, there is a consistent and emphatic message and purpose throughout Paul's letter to Titus that is aptly expressed in the title, "Exhort and Reprove to Commendable Works according to the Hope of Eternal Life."

AUTHORSHIP, AUDIENCE AND HISTORICAL
SETTING OF THE LETTER

Most critical scholars today hold that Titus was not written by the historical Paul.[3] They conclude that Titus, along with 1 and 2 Timothy, is pseudonymous and represents a second-century church setting in which Christ's return no longer yields significant influence on believers, thus resulting in a domesticated Christianity.[4] Some notable commentators, however, have challenged the mainstream position by insisting that the historical apostle Paul was the actual author of the Pastorals.[5] Howard Marshall opts for a third position—"allonymity."[6] He argues that a student of the apostle either edited the notes of his deceased teacher or carried

3. For a summary of the main arguments against Pauline authorship, see Dibelius and Conzelmann, *A Commentary on the Pastoral Epistles*, 1–5.

4. For further discussion on pseudonymity, see Bauckham, "Pseudo-Apostolic Letters," 469–94; Norbert Brox, "Zu den persönlichen Notizen der Pastoralbrief," 76–94; Dunn, *The Living Word*, 82.

5. See, e.g., the following commentaries: Mounce, *Pastoral Epistles*; Fee, *1 and 2 Timothy, Titus*; Knight, *The Pastoral Epistles*.

6. Marshall, *Pastoral Epistles*, 83–84.

the apostle's theology to the next generation. This position, according to Marshall, accounts for some of the Pastorals' linguistic distinctives while explaining some common theological themes.[7] I do not take a position regarding historical authorship because it is impossible to "prove" the authenticity of the letter. Moreover, my concern is for the implied author who is to be understood by the implied audience as the historical apostle.

The implied author "Paul" (1:1) sent the letter to Titus after leaving him in Crete to appoint elders in every town (1:5) and to deal with agitators who were teaching "what is not necessary" (1:11). Verse 3:12 suggests that Paul is not in captivity and intends to reunite with his colleague at Nicopolis in the coming winter. More importantly, Paul views himself as "a slave of God and apostle of Christ Jesus" (1:1), i.e., as one who is uniquely entrusted with the word of God (1:3). This last observation is important because it reflects the author's expectation of obedience on the part of the audience.

The second person plural "you" of 3:16 indicates that the implied audience consist not only of Titus, but also of the Cretan Christians. The implied author seemed to have written the letter knowing that it would be read to a "greater" audience. After all, why else would Paul write such an extensive introduction regarding his apostleship, highlight his apostolic authority throughout the letter, use language that would resonate with (and unsettle) a Cretan audience, and, in general, apply a persuasive rhetorical strategy if he were simply writing to an individual, let alone a trusted colleague? Moreover, even if the letter were addressed primarily to Titus, it does not concern only Titus. It concerns his relationship to the Cretan community. If it were a purely private letter, how were its contents to be made known to the Cretan church and why do we have it in the NT? Titus would either have to relay the information in his own words, or, as seems much more likely, have the letter read to the Cretans. Thus, Paul's letter to Titus is to be interpreted as a communal letter with the implied audience including Titus and the Cretan believers.

Paul's undisputed letters indicate that the apostle considered Titus to be a trustworthy partner for gospel ministry. Galatians 2:3 suggests that Titus became Paul's companion early on in his ministry. In the Corinthian catastrophe, Titus represented Paul in rectifying the situation in Corinth

7. Although some scholars protest the use of the term "Pastorals" (e.g., Towner, *Letters*, 88), it is the traditional name for the three letters and will, for conventional purposes, be used in this book.

and overseeing the collection for poor believers (2 Cor 2:3–4, 13; 7:6–16; 8:16–24). In the letter addressed to him, Titus maintains this consistent position as Paul's representative tasked to appoint future church leaders and to reprove false teachers.

An island located in the Mediterranean Sea, south of Greece and west of Asia Minor, Crete was one of the last strongholds to come under Roman rule in 71 BCE, though the extent of Roman influence is still unclear.[8] Situated ideally for sea trade and even piracy, it was a place of debauchery, violence, gluttony, and duplicity (see 1:12). At the same time, it naturally became a seedbed for philosophy, culture, and religion. While this was not uncommon for Roman provinces, Crete distinguished itself through its retelling of the story of Zeus. Cretans made the claim of being the guardians of Zeus's birthplace and tomb on Mount Ida. In addition, greedy Cretan orators often made a living from smooth public speaking and teaching in households (see 1:10–11). Thus, Cretans, consistent with the infamy of Zeus, earned the reputation of being proud liars.[9] The emphasis in Titus on sincerity and the letter's description of God as the one "who cannot lie" (1:2) fit well with this historical situation concerning Crete.

Key phrases in Titus—"those of the circumcision" (1:10), "quarrels about the law" (3:9)—suggest not only the presence of Judaism but also the influence Jewish-Christians teachers had in the churches of Crete. In contrast to the apostle and his emissary, these teachers maintained the avaricious Cretan system of teaching for selfish gain. With this background the present study will assume that the implied audience were familiar with elements from Greco-Roman culture, Judaism, and Christianity.[10]

LITERARY-RHETORICAL, AUDIENCE-ORIENTED APPROACH

In addition to doubting the Pauline authorship of the letter, various scholars have argued that Titus is a composite letter, possessing little—if any—literary unity and integrity.[11] Recent studies, however, have challenged

8. Wieland, "Roman Crete and the Letter to Titus," 339–40. For a collection of background information sources on Crete and the Cretans, see Towner, *Letters*, 659–62.

9. Ibid., 345.

10. Outside of this historical situation, it is difficult to make sense of some of the unique features of the letter. See Wieland, "Roman Crete and the Letter to Titus," 354.

11. See, e.g., Miller, *The Pastoral Letters as Composite Documents*; Guthrie, *The Pastoral Epistles*; Hanson, *Studies in the Pastoral Epistles*; Easton, *The Pastoral Epistles*.

this position.[12] Following this latter trend, I treat Titus as a single, unified letter. In addition, the chiastic structures that I will propose for the letter strengthen the position for literary integrity and unity.

Titus, then, is to be understood as a single and coherent letter written to be performed in a communal setting (most likely in a liturgical assembly) as a substitute for Paul's actual presence.[13] The proposed study will apply to Titus a text-centered, literary-rhetorical, and audience-oriented method. "Text-centered" means paying attention to what is actually contained and expressed in the text versus speculations concerning what the author intended to say or include. "Literary-rhetorical" means that Titus falls under the literary genre of a "letter" with the rhetorical purpose of persuading the implied audience to the perspective of Paul, the implied author, i.e., the author indicated in the text.[14] "Audience-oriented" indicates an interpretive approach that seeks to determine how the implied audience are required to respond to Paul's exhortations as they are strategically revealed throughout the chiastic progression of the letter.[15]

12. The same is true for 1 and 2 Timothy. Marshall, "The Christology of Luke-Acts and the Pastoral Epistles," 171: "There is a growing body of evidence that the Pastoral Epistles are not a conglomerate of miscellaneous ideas roughly thrown together with no clear plan, purpose or structure. On the contrary, they demonstrate signs of a coherent structure and of theological competence." See, e.g., Donelson, "The Structure of Ethical Argument in the Pastorals," 108; Towner, "Pauline Theology or Pauline Tradition," 288; Classen, "A Rhetorical Reading of the Epistle to Titus," 427–44; Wendland, "'Let No One Disregard You,'" 334–51; Van Neste, *Cohesion and Structure in the Pastoral Epistles*, 234–82.

13. For more information on the oral performance of the NT documents, see Shiner, *Proclaiming the Gospel*; concerning Paul's letters specifically, see Botha, "Verbal Art," 409–28; Stirewalt, *Paul the Letter Writer*, 13–18; Richards, *Paul and First-Century Letter Writing*, 202.

14. With regard to the literary genre of Titus, some—comparing it to 1 Timothy—have proposed that it is a "church order letter." While Titus 1:5 reflects some concern for church order, this designation fails to capture the overarching theme and tone of the letter, which I have summarized as "Exhort and Reprove to Commendable Works according to the Hope of Eternal Life."

15. For more on the audience-oriented method in recent biblical studies, see Carter and Heil, *Matthew's Parables*, 8–17; Heil, *The Meal Scenes in Luke-Acts*, 2–4; idem, *The Transfiguration of Jesus*.

SUMMARY

1. In this book I propose and will demonstrate new chiastic structures for the entire letter to Titus as a key to understanding it as a call to exhort and reprove to commendable works according to the hope of eternal life.

2. Although the Pauline authorship of Titus continues to be challenged, Paul, the historical apostle, is to be understood as the implied author. Titus and the Cretan Christians make up the implied audience.

3. I employ a text-centered, literary-rhetorical and audience-oriented method concerned with demonstrating how the implied audience are persuaded by the dynamic progression of the letter's chiastic structures to exhort and reprove one another.

2

The Chiastic Structures of Titus

THE FOUR MICROCHIASTIC UNITS OF THE LETTER[1]

CHIASTIC PATTERNS ORGANIZE THE content to be heard. In this way, they help both the performer and implied audience recall and follow the content. A chiasm works by leading the audience through introductory elements to a pivotal point (or points) and then reaches its conclusion by recalling and developing, via the chiastic parallels, aspects of the introductory elements. The original audience may not have been intentional about noting and pondering over such chiasms given they were fairly common in ancient oral-auricular and rhetorical cultures.[2] Rather, they experienced these dynamic chiastic patterns unconsciously, which had a subtle but intentional impact on the way they heard and responded to the content.[3] But the identification, delineation, and articulation of such chiastic structures in ancient documents can aid modern interpreters of the text who are unaccustomed to and unaware of such literary devices.[4]

In order to be credible a proposed extended chiastic structure must be based on a meticulous and rigorous methodology. The methodology must demonstrate that the chiasm exists and operates objectively within the text. My investigation follows seven criteria:[5]

1. The first section of this chapter follows in large part Heil, *Philippians*, 10–13.

2. See Brouwer, *The Literary Development of John 13–17*, 23–27; White, "Apostolic Mission and Apostolic Message," 157.

3. Dewey, "Mark as Aural Narrative: Structures as Clues to Understanding," 50–52.

4. On the interpretive significance of chiastic structures, see Breck, "Biblical Chiasmus: Exploring Structure for Meaning," 70–74; Longenecker, *Rhetoric at the Boundaries*, 16–17, 22–23; Man, "The Value of Chiasm for New Testament Interpretation," 146–57.

5. See also Blomberg, "The Structure of 2 Corinthians 1–7," 4–8; Jeremias, "Chiasms

1. There must be problems in recognizing the structure of the text in consideration, which traditional outlines have not been able to resolve.

2. There must be indications of parallelism and pendulum movements in the text that commentaries and specialized studies have already observed.

3. Chiasms must be demonstrated to exist in the received text and do not require unsupported and excessive textual emendations for substantiation.

4. Precise verbal parallelism—supported by conceptual and syntactical parallels—should link the corresponding pairs.

5. Such verbal parallelism should involve significant terminology versus peripheral language and should be unique to the parallel units.

6. The pivot, i.e., the center of the chiasm, should function as the turning point in the literary structure.

7. A corollary to the fourth observation is that chiasms must always be "framed," i.e., parallel units must gravitate around the pivot.

The key feature of this study is that all of the proposed chiasms are based on precise linguistic parallels in the text, including cognates, synonyms, antonyms, alliterative terms, and, on occasion, an identical grammatical form of a word. Some of the linguistic parallels involve seemingly ordinary words to a modern audience, but these may have been significant to the rhetorical strategy of the author and the situation of the original audience.

Since the proposed chiasms are based on linguistic parallels, they may not exhibit a balance in the length of the parallel elements or units, i.e., one parallel element or unit may be longer or shorter than its corresponding parallel. While this asymmetry may seem unusual to a contemporary audience, an ancient audience would have been attuned to the key linguistic parallels as the letter to Titus was performed rather than to a balance in the length of the parallels. The main presupposition of this study is that there is an operative chiasm—irrespective of "balance"—if linguistic parallels with a pivotal section between them are evident.

---

in den Paulusbriefen," 145–56; Welch, "Criteria for Identifying and Evaluating the Presence of Chiasmus," 154–74; Thomson, *Chiasmus in the Pauline Letters*, 13–45.

Furthermore, the proposed chiasms may not have the same number of elements or units. Some exhibit a single central element, e.g., A-B-C-B'-A', while others exhibit dual elements, e.g., A-B-C-C'-B'-A'. Both types operate as chiasms since they involve a movement from the first to the second half of the chiasm. In addition, it is better to describe the central element or elements as the pivot of the chiasm and the final A' element as the climax. This is an important observation, given chiasms are not merely circular or repetitive arguments, but dynamic literary patterns, progressing and developing the meaning of the linguistic parallels.

In the rest of this chapter, I will first demonstrate how the text of Paul's letter to Titus organizes itself into four distinct literary units, microchiastic structures determined by linguistic parallels found objectively in the text. Then I will demonstrate how these four units form a macrochiastic pattern, also determined by linguistic parallels found objectively in the text. Finally, I will note the transitional words that occur at the conclusion of one unit and at the beginning of the next unit. These indicate that the chiastic units are to be heard sequentially and are capitalized in the translations below.[6]

Paul to Titus according to Faith on the Basis of the Hope of Eternal Life (1:1–4)[7]

A. [1a] Paul, slave of God (θεοῦ) and apostle of Jesus Christ ('Ιησοῦ Χριστοῦ) according to the faith (πίστιν) of the elect of God (θεοῦ)

B. [1b] and the recognition of the truth that is according to godliness, [2a] on the basis of the hope of eternal (αἰωνίου) life

C. [2b] that God, who cannot lie, promised

B'. [2c] before eternal (αἰωνίων) ages

A'. [3] and revealed at the proper time his word in the proclamation with which I was considered faithful (ἐπιστεύθην) according to the command

---

6. All translations of the subsequent units of the letter are mine. Every effort has been made to be as literal as possible to the Greek text for the purposes of clarifying the exegesis that will follow.

7. The opening of Titus is longer and more elaborate than the openings of most of the other letters attributed to Paul (vv. 1–4 form a single sentence in the Greek). The extended opening captures key themes (e.g., "godliness," "hope," "salvation") that the apostle will expand on in the letter. Their appearance in the introduction invites the audience to pay careful attention to them in the rest of the letter (see Johnson, *Letters*, 217).

of God (θεοῦ) our savior. 4 To Titus, true child according to a common faith (πίστιν): GRACE and peace from God (θεοῦ) the Father and Christ Jesus (Χριστοῦ Ἰησοῦ) our savior.[8]

Directed to "Titus, true child according to a common faith," the prayer wish, "Grace and peace from God the Father and Christ Jesus our savior" in Titus 1:1–4 is set off grammatically from 1:5–13a, which is a reminder to appoint elders. The integrity of this first unit is further established by the A-B-C-B'-A' chiastic structure. The quadruple occurrences of the genitive "God" (θεοῦ)[9] and the double occurrences of "Jesus Christ" (Ἰησοῦ Χριστοῦ)[10] and "faith" (πίστιν)[11] determine the parallelism of the A (1:1a) and A' (1:3–4) elements of the chiasm. The double occurrences of the genitive "eternal"—"eternal (αἰωνίου) life" in 1:2a and "eternal (αἰωνίων) ages" in 1:2c—determine the parallelism of the B (1:1b–2a) and B' (1:2c) elements. The unique occurrence, both in this unit and in the entire letter, of the adjective "cannot lie" (ἀψευδής) in 1:2b distinguishes the C element as the unparalleled pivot of the first unit. All of the aforementioned parallel words are unique to their respective elements and do not appear elsewhere in the unit.

Exhort with Sound Doctrine and Reprove Opponents (1:5–13a)

A. [5] For this REASON (χάριν) I left you in Crete (Κρήτη), so that what is left you might set right and appoint, according to city, elders, as I directed you, [6] if one (τις) is blameless, husband of one wife, having faithful children not in accusation of debauchery or rebellious (ἀνυπότακτα). [7] For it is necessary (δεῖ) that the overseer be blameless, as a household-manager (οἰκονόμον) of God, not arrogant, not irritable, not a drunkard, not bel-

8. For different proposals concerning the structure of the opening, see Marshall, *Pastoral Epistles*, 114; Towner, *Letters*, 664. Their structures, which include only the first three verses, highlight Paul's role in God's plan of redemption but do not do full justice to the connections between Paul, Titus, and the audience, which are central to appreciating the arrangement and function of the letter's introduction.

9. The word "God" (θεός) occurs in 1:2b but is distinct from its occurrences in 1:1a and 1:3–4 because it occurs in the nominative as the subject of the clause.

10. The order of "Jesus Christ" (Ἰησοῦ Χριστου) in 1:1a is reversed to "Christ Jesus" (Χριστοῦ Ἰησοῦ) in 1:4. This alternation reinforces the chiasm through the arrangement "Jesus-Christ-Christ-Jesus."

11. The occurrence of the verb ἐπιστεύθην in 1:3 further strengthens the parallelism of the A and A' elements.

ligerent, not greedy for shameful gain (αἰσχροκερδῆ); ⁸ rather a lover-of-strangers, a lover-of-goodness, sensible, just, devout, self-controlled,

B. ⁹ᵃ holding fast (ἀντεχόμενον) to the faithful word (λόγου) that is according to the teaching (διδαχήν),

B'. ⁹ᵇ so that he might be able both to exhort with sound doctrine (διδασκαλίᾳ) and reprove those who oppose (ἀντιλέγοντας).

A'. ¹⁰ For there are many rebels (ἀνυπότακτοι), empty-talkers and deceivers, especially the circumcision, ¹¹ whom it is necessary (δεῖ) to silence, who are upsetting whole households (οἴκους), teaching what is not necessary (δεῖ) for this reason (χάριν)—shameful gain (αἰσχροῦ κέρδους). ¹² One (τις) of THEM, THEIR own prophet, said, "Cretans (Κρῆτες) are always liars, evil beasts, lazy gluttons." ¹³ᵃ THIS testimony is true.¹²

The preposition χάριν in the expression "For this reason" that introduces this unit in 1:5 recalls "grace" (χάρις) at the beginning of the prayer wish in 1:4 that concludes the preceding unit. These terms serve as the transitional words linking the first unit (1:1–4) to the second unit (1:5–13a).

An A-B-B'-A' chiastic pattern secures the integrity and distinctiveness of this second unit (1:5–13a). The obvious contrast between the elders (1:5–9) and the rebels (1:10–13a) further supports the integrity of this unit: each group's identity is defined by its antithesis. This particular chiasm introduces the letter's rhetorical intention to have the audience consider whether they are for or against Paul (1:1–4; 3:15), whether they are like the elders who are characterized by commendable works (1:5–9; 2:1–3:8) or like the false teachers who are unfit for any good work (1:10–16; 3:9–11).

The double occurrences of the preposition χάριν in 1:5 and 1:11 serve as parallels for the A (1:5–8) and A' (1:10–13a) elements of the chiasm. The cognates "Crete" and "Cretans"—"For this reason I left you in Crete (Κρήτῃ)" in 1:5 and "Cretans (Κρῆτες) are always liars" in 1:12, and "household-manager" (οἰκονόμον) in 1:7 and "households" (οἴκους) in

12. Verse 13a is included in this microchiasm because of the connection between the two forms of the verb "to be" (εἰμί) in 1:10 (εἰσίν) and 1:13a (ἐστίν).

There are lengthy additions after the endings of 1:9 and 1:11 in a trilingual manuscript of the thirteenth century (460). These additions are later, reflecting knowledge of 1 and 2 Timothy; see *TCGNT*, 584–85. Also, after χάριν (1:12), the trilingual manuscript 460 adds: "the children who mistreat or strike their own parents you must reprove and admonish as a father his children."

1:11—strengthen the chiasm. The double occurrences of "one"—"if one (τίς) is blameless" in 1:6 and "one (τίς) of them" in 1:12, of the adjective "rebellious"—"in accusation of debauchery or rebellious (ἀνυπότακτα)" in 1:6 and "For there are many rebels (ἀνυπότακτοι)" in 1:10, and of the phrase "shameful gain"—not "greedy for shameful gain" (αἰσχροκερδῆ) in 1:7 and for "shameful gain" (αἰσχροῦ κέρδους) in 1:11—further contribute to the parallelism. Finally, the triple occurrences of the verb "it is necessary"—"For it is necessary (δεῖ) that the overseer be blameless" in 1:7 and "whom it is necessary (δεῖ) to silence" and "teaching what is not necessary (δεῖ)" in 1:11—confirm the parallelism. All of the above parallel words are unique to the A and A' elements of the unit and do not occur anywhere else in the letter.

The assonances "holding fast" (ἀντεχόμενον) and "word" (λόγου) in 1:9a and "those who oppose" (ἀντιλέγοντας) in 1:9b, and the cognates "teaching" (διδαχήν) in 1:9a and "doctrine" (διδασκαλίᾳ) in 1:9b, determine the parallelism between the B (1:9a) and B' (1:9b) elements of the chiasm. The B-B' parallelism forms the pivot of the second microchiasm, grammatically distinguished from the A-A' parallelism through its use of participles (1:9a) versus adjectives (1:7–8, 10). While the terms "word" (λόγος), "doctrine" (διδασκαλία), and "those who oppose" (ἀντιλέγοντας) occur elsewhere in the letter, they are unique to the B-B' elements in this second microchiasm.

Reprove and Exhort with Sound Doctrine as We Await Our Savior (1:13b–3:3)

A. ¹³ᵇ Therefore, reprove (ἔλεγχε) THEM severely, so that they might be sound in the faith, ¹⁴ not paying attention to Jewish myths and commands of human beings (ἀνθρώπων) who turn away the truth. ¹⁵ All things are clean to the clean. But to the defiled and unfaithful nothing is clean; rather, defiled are both their mind and conscience. ¹⁶ God they profess to know but by their works they deny, being vile and disobedient (ἀπειθεῖς) and unqualified for all good work (πρὸς πᾶν ἔργον ἀγαθόν).

B. ²:¹ But you speak (λάλει) what is consistent with sound doctrine. ² Older men are to be temperate, serious, sensible, sound in faith, in love, in endurance. ³ Older women, similarly, are to be reverent in behavior, not slanderers, not enslaved to much wine, commendable teachers 4 so that they may make sensible the younger women to be lovers-of-husbands, lovers-of-children, ⁵ sensible, chaste, homemakers, good, submitting to their own husbands, so that the word of God might not be blasphemed. ⁶ Exhort (παρακάλει) the younger men to be similarly sensible ⁷ about all things, presenting yourself as a model of commendable works (καλῶν ἔργων), in the doctrine incorruption, seriousness, ⁸ sound word that is beyond reproach, so that the opponent may be put to shame, having (ἔχων) nothing bad to say about us (περὶ ἡμῶν). ⁹ Slaves are to submit to their own masters in all things, to be pleasing, not those who oppose, ¹⁰ᵃ not those who pilfer; rather those who demonstrate that all faith is good,

> C. ¹⁰ᵇ so that they might adorn the doctrine of God our savior (σωτῆρος) in all things. ¹¹ For the grace of God has appeared (ἐπεφάνη), saving (σωτήριος) all human beings, ¹² training us, so that by denying ungodliness and worldly desires we may live sensibly and righteously and godly in the present age,

> D. ¹³ᵃ awaiting the blessed hope,

> C'. ¹³ᵇ the appearance (ἐπιφάνειαν) of the glory of our great God and savior (σωτῆρος) Jesus Christ,

B'. ¹⁴ who gave himself on behalf of us (ὑπὲρ ἡμῶν), so that he might redeem us from all lawlessness and cleanse for himself a special people, zealous for commendable works (καλῶν ἔργων). ¹⁵ᵃ These things speak (λάλει) and exhort (παρακάλει)

A'. ¹⁵ᵇ and reprove (ἔλεγχε) with all command; let no one disregard you. ³:¹ Remind them to submit to ruling authorities, to be obedient, to be ready for all good work (πρὸς πᾶν ἔργον ἀγαθόν), ² to blaspheme no one, to be unquarrelsome, kind, demonstrating all gentleness towards all HUMAN BEINGS (ἀνθρώπους). ³ For we too were once ignorant, disobedient (ἀπειθεῖς), misled, enslaved to various desires and pleasures, spending our lives in evil and envy, despicable, hating one another.

The pronoun "them" (αὐτούς) in the command "reprove them severely" in 1:13b at the beginning of this unit recalls the pronoun's double occurrences of αὐτῶν in 1:12 and single occurrence of αὕτη in 1:13a. These occurrences of the pronoun thus serve as the transitional words linking the second unit (1:5–13a) to the third unit (1:13b–3:3).

An A-B-C-D-C'-B'-A' chiastic pattern secures the integrity and distinctness of the third unit of the letter. The only two occurrences in the letter of the imperative form of the verb "to reprove"—"reprove (ἔλεγχε) them severely" in 1:13b and "reprove (ἔλεγχε) with all command" in 2:15b—initiate the parallelism of the A (1:13b-16) and the A' (2:15b-3:3) elements. The double occurrences of the plural form for "human beings"—"commandments of human beings (ἀνθρώπων)" in 1:14 and "for all human beings (ἀνθρώπους)" in 3:2—further supports the parallelism. Finally, the only two occurrences in the letter of the adjective "disobedient" (ἀπειθεῖς) in 1:16 and 3:3, and of the exact phrase "for all good work" (πρὸς πᾶν ἔργον ἀγαθόν) in 1:16 and in 3:1 establish the parallelism of the A and A' elements of the third microchiasm. These parallel terms and phrases are unique to the A-A' elements of the third unit.

The only occurrences in the letter of the imperative form of the verb "to speak"—"But speak (λάλει) what is consistent" in 2:1 and "These things speak (λάλει)" in 2:15a—serve as parallels for the B (2:1-10a) and B' (2:14-15a) elements. In addition, the only occurrences in the letter of the imperative form of the verb "to exhort"—"Similarly, exhort (παρακάλει) the younger men" in 2:6 and "These things speak and exhort (παρακάλει)" in 2:15a—strengthen the parallelism. The double occurrences of the phrase "commendable works"—"a model of commendable works (καλῶν ἔργων)" in 2:7 and "zealous for commendable works (καλῶν ἔργων)" in 2:14,[13] and the assonances "about us" (περὶ ἡμῶν) in 2:8 and "for us" (ὑπὲρ ἡμῶν) in 2:14—establish the parallelism of the B and B' elements of the third micro-chiasm. While the word "work" (ἔργον) occurs both in the A-A' (ἔργον ἀγαθόν in 1:16 and 3:1) and B-B' elements (καλῶν ἔργων in 2:7 and 2:14), they do not operate as parallels because of their differing adjectives. All of the aforementioned parallel terms and phrases occur uniquely in the B and B' units of the macrochiasm.

The C and C' elements share two linguistic connections. The double occurrences of the genitive "savior"—"the doctrine of God our savior

---

13. In 1:16 "work" is qualified by the adjective ἀγαθόν. Paul, however, uses the adjective καλῶν in 2:7b to describe "works." Thus, although the *NAB*, *ESV*, and *NET* do not note the distinction in their translations, it is necessary to use a different term (hence, "commendable") in order to consider the possible nuance that the apostle has in mind. The translation "commendable" expresses also the standard definition "being in accordance at a high level . . . good, useful"; with respect to moral quality, "praiseworthy" (BDAG, s.v.).

(σωτῆρος)" in 2:10b and "our great God and savior (σωτῆρος) Jesus Christ" in 2:13b—serve as parallels for the C (2:10b-12) and C' (2:13b) elements. While the word in its genitive form is found elsewhere in the letter (1:3, 4; 3:4, 6), within this unit it occurs uniquely in the C and C' elements. The single occurrence in the letter of the adjective "saving" (σωτήριος) in 2:11 strengthens this linguistic connection. The cognates "to appear" and "appearing"—"the grace of God has appeared (ἐπεφάνη)" in 2:11 and "the appearance (ἐπιφάνειαν) of the glory of our great God" in 2:13b—further establish the parallelism. While the verb "to appear" occurs once more in 3:4, the noun "appearing" occurs only once in the letter. The unparalleled, central, and pivotal D element (2:13a) element contains the only occurrence of the words "awaiting" (προσδεχόμενοι) and "blessed" (μακαρίαν) in the letter.

Justified by Grace in Faith according to the Hope of Eternal Life (3:4–15)

A. ⁴ But when the kindness and the love-for-HUMAN-BEINGS (φιλανθρωπία) of God our savior appeared, ⁵ not from works that we did in righteousness; rather, according to his mercy he saved us through the washing of rebirth and renewal of the Holy Spirit, ⁶ whom he poured out on us richly through Jesus Christ our savior, ⁷ so that being made righteous by his grace (χάριτι) we might become heirs according to the hope of eternal life. ⁸ᵃ Faithful (πιστός) is the word, and about these things I want you to insist, so that those who have faith in (πεπιστευκότες) God may be intent to engage in commendable works (καλῶν ἔργων προΐστασθαι).

   B. ⁸ᵇ These are commendable and useful (ὠφέλιμα) to human beings. ⁹ᵃ But avoid foolish inquiries and genealogies and rivalries and quarrels about the law (νομικάς),

   B'. ⁹ᵇ for they are useless (ἀνωφελεῖς) and empty. ¹⁰ After a first and second warning dismiss a heretical human being, ¹¹ knowing that such a person is perverted and sinning, being self-decided. ¹² When I send Artemas to you or Tychicus, hasten to come to me at Nicopolis, for I have decided to winter there. ¹³ Zenas the lawyer (νομικόν) and Apollos hastily send, so that nothing is lacking for them.

A'. ¹⁴ And let our own also learn to engage in commendable works (καλῶν ἔργων προΐστασθαι) for urgent needs, so that they might not be unfruitful. [15] All who are with me greet you. Greet those who love (φιλοῦ ντας) us in the faith (πίστει). Grace (χάρις) be with all of you.

The word "love-for-human-beings" (φιλανθρωπία) in the phrase "the love-for-human-beings of God our savior" in 3:4 at the beginning of this unit recalls "human beings" (ἀνθρώπους) at the conclusion of the preceding unit (3:2).[14] These slight variations of "human being" thus serve as the transitional words linking the third unit (1:13b—3:3) and the fourth unit (3:4–15).

An A-B-B'-A' chiastic pattern secures the integrity and distinctness of this final unit. The assonances—"when the kindness and the love-for-human-beings (φιλανθρωπία) of God our savior" in 3:4 and "those who love (φιλοῦντας) us" in 3:15—serve as parallels for the A (3:4–8a) and A' (3:14–15) elements of the chiasm. The repetition of the related terms—"Faithful (πιστός) is the word" and "those who have faith" (πεπιστευκότες) in 3:8a, and "those who love us in the faith (πίστει)" in 3:15—provides additional linguistic support for the parallelism. The double occurrences of "grace"—"by his grace" (χάριτι) in 3:7 and "Grace (χάρις) be with all of you" in 3:15, and the double occurrences of the exact clause "to engage in commendable works" (καλῶν ἔργων προΐστασθαι) in 3:8a and in 3:14—establish the parallelism.[15] All of the above parallel terms and phrases are unique to the A and A' elements and do not occur elsewhere in the unit.

The B and B' elements of the fourth chiasm also evidence strong linguistic connections. The contrasting adjectives "useful" and "useless"— "These are commendable and useful (ὠφέλιμα)" in 3:8b and "for they are useless (ἀνωφελεῖς) and empty" in 3:9b—serve as parallels for the B (3:8b–9a) and B' (3:9b–13) elements. The double occurrences of "human beings"—"useful to human beings (ἀνθρώποις)" in 3:8b and "a

---

14. The *NAB* translates φιλανθρωπία as "generous love"; *ESV* "loving kindness"; *NET* "his love." The translation "love-for-human beings" not only represents a more literal translation of the Greek but is also consistent with earlier translations for φιλόξενον ("lover-of-strangers") and φιλάγαθον ("lover-of-goodness") in 1:8 and φιλάνδρους ("lovers-of-husbands") and φιλοτέκνους ("lovers-of-children") in 2:4. This consistency in translation highlights the link between God's "love-for-human beings" and the impact it should have on the "elect" (1:1a) in effecting the qualities "lover-of-strangers," "lover-of-goodness," "lovers-of-husbands," and "lovers-of-children."

15. In addition, the occurrence of "works" (ἔργων) in 3:5 strengthens this particular connection.

heretical human being (ἄνθρωπον)" in 3:10, and of the adjective "law"—
"genealogies and rivalries and quarrels about the law (νομικάς)" in 3:9a
and "Zenas, the lawyer (νομικόν)" in 3:13—determine the parallelism of
the B and B' elements. All of these parallel terms are unique to the B and
B' elements and do not occur elsewhere in the unit.

THE MACROCHIASTIC STRUCTURE OF THE LETTER

Having demonstrated the various microchiastic structures operative in
the four distinct units of the letter to Titus, I will now show how these
four units form an A-B-B'-A' macrochiastic structure organizing the entire letter.

A. [1:1-4:] Paul to Titus according to Faith on the Basis of the Hope of Eternal
Life

A'. [3:4-15:] Justified by Grace in Faith according to the Hope of Eternal Life

The A and A' units of the macrochiasm are connected by several
sets of parallel terms and phrases. The "hope of eternal life" (ἐλπίδι
ζωῆς αἰωνίου) in 1:2a of the A unit parallels the "hope of eternal life"
(ἐλπίδα ζωῆς αἰωνίου) in 3:7 of the A' unit.[16] The identification of believers as "those who have faith (πεπιστευκότες) in God" (3:8a) in the
A' unit recalls Paul's self-description as one who "was considered faithful
(ἐπιστεύθην) according to the command of God" (1:3) in the A unit.
The phrase "Christ Jesus our savior" (Χριστοῦ Ἰησοῦ τοῦ σωτῆρος
ἡμῶν) in 1:4 of the A unit parallels the phrase "Jesus Christ our savior"
(Ἰησοῦ Χριστοῦ τοῦ σωτῆρος ἡμῶν) in 3:6 of the A' unit. All of the
aforementioned parallel terms and phrases occur uniquely in the A and
A' units of the macrochiasm.

B. [1:5-13a:] Exhort with Sound Doctrine and Reprove Opponents

B'. [1:13b-3:3:] Reprove and Exhort with Sound Doctrine as We Await Our
Savior

The B and B' units of the macrochiasm are connected by multiple
sets of parallel terms and phrases. The "husband (ἀνήρ) of one wife" in
1:6 of the B unit parallels "submitting to their own husbands (ἀνδράσιν)"

16. The occurrence of the adjective "eternal" (αἰωνίων) in 1:2c of the A unit strengthens this particular connection.

in 2:5 of the B' unit. "Having (ἔχων) faithful children" in 1:6 of the B unit parallels "having (ἔχων) nothing to say" in 2:8 of the B' unit.

Appointing "sensible" (σώφρονα) elders in 1:8 of the B unit parallels exhorting various members of God's household to be "sensible" in 2:2 (σώφρονας), 2:5 (σώφρονας), and 2:6 (σωφρονεῖν) of the B' unit. The elders' calling to exhort (παρακαλεῖν) in 1:9b of the B unit parallels Titus's calling to exhort in 2:6 (παρακάλει) and 2:15a (παρακάλει) of the B' unit. "To exhort in sound doctrine (τῇ διδασκαλίᾳ τῇ ὑγιαινούσῃ)" in 1:9b of the B unit parallels "But speak what befits sound doctrine (ὑγιαινούσῃ διδασκαλίᾳ)" in 2:1 of the B' unit. "Teaching" (διδαχήν) in 1:9a and "doctrine" (διδασκαλίᾳ) in 1:9b of the B unit parallel the triple occurrences of "doctrine" in 2:1 (διδασκαλία), 2:7 (διδασκαλία), and 2:10b (διδασκαλίαν) and the single occurrence of "commendable teachers" (καλοδιδασκάλους) in 2:3 of the B' unit. The qualifier "sound" (ὑγιαινούσῃ) in 1:9b of the B unit parallels the triple occurrences of "sound" in 1:13b (ὑγιαίνωσιν), 2:1 (ὑγιαινούσῃ), and 2:2 (ὑγιαίνοντας) of the B' unit. Refuting "those who oppose" (ἀντιλέγοντας) in 1:9b of the B unit parallels the exhortation to "those who oppose" (ἀντιλέγοντας) in 2:9 of the B' unit. Finally, the elders' calling "to reprove" (ἐλέγχειν) in 1:9b of the B unit parallels the double occurrences of the apostle's command to "reprove" in 1:13b (ἔλεγχε) and 2:15b (ἔλεγχε) of the B' unit.

All of these aforementioned parallel terms occur uniquely in the B and B' units of the macrochiasm.

OUTLINE OF THE MACROCHIASTIC STRUCTURE OF THE LETTER

A. 1:1-4: Paul to Titus according to Faith on the Basis of the Hope of Eternal Life

B. 1:5-13a: Exhort with Sound Doctrine and Reprove Opponents

B'. 1:13b-3:3: Reprove and Exhort with Sound Doctrine as We Await Our Savior

A'. 3:4-15: Justified by Grace in Faith according to the Hope of Eternal Life

SUMMARY

1. To substantiate an extended chiastic structure for the entire letter to Titus a thorough, consistent, and detailed methodology is necessary and has been provided.

2. There are four distinct units in the letter to Titus with each exhibiting its own microchiastic structures.

3. The four units comprising Titus form a macrochiastic structure with two pairs of parallel units.

3

Titus 1:1–4: Paul to Titus according to Faith on the Basis of the Hope of Eternal Life (A)

A. [1a] Paul, slave of *God* and apostle of *Jesus Christ* according to the *faith* of the elect of *God*

   B. [1b] and the recognition of the truth that is according to godliness, [2a] on the basis of the hope of *eternal* life

      C. [2b] that God, who cannot lie, promised

   B'. [2c] before *eternal* ages

A'. [3] and revealed at the proper time his word in the proclamation with which I was considered *faithful* according to the command of *God* our savior. [4] To Titus, true child according to a common *faith*: Grace and peace from *God* the Father and *Christ Jesus* our savior.[1]

AUDIENCE RESPONSE TO TITUS 1:1–4

Titus 1:1a (A): Paul, Slave of God and Apostle of Jesus Christ

IN TITUS 1:1A THE audience members hear the A element of the first chiastic unit (1:1–4) as a mini-chiasm in itself. Verse 1a is composed carefully of three balanced and rhythmic sub-elements:

   a. Paul, slave of God (θεοῦ)

      b. and apostle of Jesus Christ

   a'. according to the faith of the elect of God (θεοῦ)

The mini-chiasm invites the audience to interpret Paul's apostolic calling in light of their own "faith": he has been commissioned as a slave of

---

1. For the establishment of Titus 1:1–4 as a chiasm, see ch. 2.

God to deepen, through this letter, the "faith" of the audience who are the "elect of God."

The "a" and "a'" sub-elements share a unique rhythmic relationship, each ending with the genitive form of "God." Together they form an *inclusio* for the mini-chiasm and secure its unity, focusing the audience's attention on God. The pivot concludes with a reference to "Jesus Christ." The close association between the terms "God" and "Jesus Christ," which is reflected in the artistic manner in which each sub-element ends, is deliberate, subtly communicating to the audience a high Christology.

Titus 1:1a (a): Paul, Slave of God

The letter begins with the author's self-identification as "Paul, slave of God."[2] That Paul is a "slave" (δοῦλος) tells the audience both that he has authority and that he is under authority. On the one hand, Paul places himself in the line of Moses, David, and other OT prophets who also were slaves of God, recipients of special revelation and thus commanding figures for the people of God.[3] On the other hand, like the Cretan slaves, Paul views himself as God's "property" whose life is to be characterized by full service and submission to God.[4] The audience, then, are to submit to Paul by receiving his letter with reverence, since he is one with authority from God.

Titus 1:1b (b): Apostle of Jesus Christ

In the "b" sub-element of the mini-chiasm, Paul continues his self-description as an "apostle of Jesus Christ." That Paul is an "apostle" (ἀπόστολος) means that he has been sent as an authorized delegate to convey a message

---

2. In some of the other undisputed Pauline epistles, Paul introduces himself as a "slave of Christ Jesus" (e.g., Rom 1:1; Gal 1:10; Phil 1:10). The shift in Titus appears deliberate: "His central concern at the outset is to anchor his ministry in the story of the covenant God—thus the emphasis on God" (Towner, *Letters*, 666).

3. See Mounce, *Pastoral Epistles*, 378. Concerning Moses, see Exod 14:31; Deut 34:5; Josh 1:2. Concerning David, see 2 Sam 7:5; 1 Kgs 3:6; Ps 35:1. For other OT prophets, see 1 Kgs 18:36; 2 Kgs 17:13; Jer 7:25. Note that all OT references come from the LXX.

4. For more on the analogy of slavery in Paul and at the time of the NT, see Margaret Y. MacDonald, "Slavery, Sexuality and House Churches," 94–113; Jennifer A. Glancy, *Slavery in Early Christianity*, 3–70; David L. Balch and Carolyn Osiek, *Families in the New Testament World*, 174–92; Ceslas Spicq, "Le Vocabulaire de l'esclavage dans le Nouveau Testament," 201–26.

on behalf of the sender.[5] That Paul is an apostle of "Jesus Christ" communicates to the audience that it is the risen Lord that has sent him to speak
to the audience. Taken with the "a" sub-element this second description
attunes the audience to hear what God and Christ Jesus will communicate
through the authorized and devoted slave-apostle.

Titus 1:1c (a'): According to the Faith of the Elect of God

In the "a'" sub-element, Paul now identifies himself for the audience as
one uniquely commissioned "according to (κατά) the faith of the elect of
God" in the "a'" sub-element. Paul's calling as a "slave of God and apostle
of Jesus Christ" accords with the "faith" that the "elect of God" already
possess. The prepositional phrase also implies that the contents of the
letter will refine and deepen their "faith."

While "faith" (πίστιν) can refer either to the act of believing or the
content of belief, the former makes more sense in the context: Paul has
been called to renew and strengthen belief in God. The designation "elect
of God" (ἐκλεκτῶν θεοῦ) reminds the audience of the OT references to
Israel as the elect people.[6] The audience perceive that just as Paul stands
in the same line as the OT prophets, so too they are members of the OT
community of faith.[7] Similarly, the repetition of "God" (θεοῦ) communicates to the audience that they, like the slave-apostle, belong to God and
thus are to conduct themselves under his lordship. Thus, the audience, the
"elect of God," sense a profound connection with Paul.

Titus 1:1b–2a (B): For the Recognition of the Truth according to Godliness

In the B element (1:1b–2a), Paul defines for the audience more precisely
the meaning of the "faith of the elect of God."[8] In addition, he states his
personal motivation for ministry. First, Paul's apostolic authority is according to the "recognition of the truth that is according to godliness."

---

5. Bühner, "ἀπόστολος," *EDNT*, 1. 142–46; Agnew, "The Origin of the NT Apostle-
Concept," 75–96. For insights into the varied use and meaning of the term in the NT as a
whole, see Barrett, *The Signs of an Apostle*; Rengstorf, *Apostleship*.

6. See, e.g., Ps 32:12; 104:43; Isa 43:20.

7. See Fee, *Titus*, 168.

8. Marshall, *Pastoral Epistles*, 121: "The second part of the goal statement explains
'the faith of God's elect' (the connective καί is epexegetic) in terms of 'the knowledge of
the truth which is in accord with godliness.'"

The noun ἐπίγνωσιν is often translated as "knowledge," but "recognition" better expresses the sense of the cognate verb, which means a "coming to" or "embracing of" the truth.[9] Thus, what is in view here is not primarily education but conversion and growth.[10] The term "truth" (ἀληθείας) was used in Greco-Roman literature to describe speech that expressed "things as they really are."[11] Cognizant of the OT and Paul's gospel, the audience now correlate "truth" with "faithfulness,"[12] especially God's faithfulness to Adam and Abraham in keeping the promise to redeem fallen humanity and bless all the nations.[13] The phrase as a whole reminds the audience of their full acceptance of Paul's gospel, which has at its center a faithful God—a God of truth. Paul's purpose in writing the letter as a slave of God and apostle of Jesus Christ is to deepen the audience's "recognition of the truth."

The audience's acceptance of the truth must be "according to godliness." For the audience the term "godliness" (εὐσέβειαν) originally meant reverence for the gods, which was expressed in veneration for traditional values and the structures that support them.[14] "Godliness" now, however, has been redefined in light of the "truth" that has been delivered through Paul; it now expresses reverence for Paul's "God" and "Jesus Christ" (1:1a). For this reason the audience recognize that "Paul is not interested in truth in an abstract or philosophical way."[15] Rather, he seeks conduct that is consistent with their knowledge of God's faithfulness and the reciprocal faithfulness that is expected from "the elect of God." In short, the audience's "recognition of the truth" should result in lives characterized by worship—a complete devotion to God and his purposes in every sphere of life.[16]

---

9. See Towner, *Letters*, 668.

10. For a fuller discussion of the phrase, see Sell, *The Knowledge of the Truth—Two Doctrines* (Frankfurt: Lang, 1982) 3–7.

11. Marshall, *Pastoral Epistles*, 122.

12. See Gen 24:48; Ps 30:6; Isa 38:3.

13. See Gen 3:1–24; 12:1–3; 15:1–21.

14. See Witherington, *Letters*, 99–102. For a summary of the history of interpretation of "godliness," see Marshall, *Pastoral Epistles*, 134–44; Towner, *Letters*, 171–75.

15. Witherington, *Letters*, 99.

16. For additional comments: on εὐσέβεια, see Angela Standhartinger, "Eusebeia in den Pastoralbriefen," 122–26; D'Angelo, "Eusebeia," 139–65; Foerster, "Eusebeia in den Pastoralbriefen," 213–18.

Second, Paul's motivation for his apostolic ministry is the "hope of eternal life."[17] "Hope" (ἐλπίς) in Pauline literature and in the NT does not indicate a desire or wish that may or may not happen. Rather, it indicates confidence in God's promise for a sure future and provides the motivation for present ethical living. The term "life" (ζωῆς), which can refer either to physical or spiritual "life," is qualified by the adjective "eternal" (αἰωνίου). The adjective frequently denotes long periods prior to creation or an attribute of God.[18] Taken together, the two words express more than just everlasting life. Recognizing "God" as the "eternal" one who existed long before creation, the audience hear the phrase "hope of eternal life" as the hope that all believers have of becoming like God and participating in his "eternal" mode of existence.

Titus 1:2b (C): The God, Who Cannot Lie, Promised

Paul establishes the reliability of the hope that he and all believers have by reminding the audience that it is "God, who cannot lie" (ὁ ἀψευδὴς θεός), who "promised" (ἐπηγγείλατο) "eternal life." The verb "promised" contains echoes of the OT, which recounts numerous instances of God promising redemption and blessing to those who trust in him.[19] Recipients of God's promises were expected, in turn, to act in covenant faithfulness. By implication then, both Paul and the audience are to give their full allegiance as "slaves" to God alone.

More important in the pivot than the verb "promised" is the adjective ἀψευδής, which is translated here as "who cannot lie." In short, God's nature establishes the reliability of his promise. While the adjective was a common Hellenistic philosophical term,[20] Jewish writers, including the biblical authors, tended to speak about God in positive terms (e.g.,

---

17. It is unclear whether the preposition ἐπί in Titus 1:2a modifies "apostle," "godliness," or everything that precedes it. Some commentators hold that the preposition ἐπί here denotes purpose; see Mounce, *Pastoral Epistles*, 277; Kelly, *Pastoral Epistles*, 277. Based on what the apostle states explicitly in his other letters concerning his ministerial hope (e.g., 1 Cor 15:19) and given the focus in 1:1–3 on Paul's ministry, it seems more appropriate to take 1:2 as an expression of Paul's own motivation; see Towner, *Letters*, 664; Knight, *Pastoral Epistles*, 284; Marshall, *Pastoral Epistles*, 123–24.

18. BDAG, s.v.

19. See Gen 18:19; 21:1; 28:15; Exod 12:25; 32:13.

20. See the multiple references in LSJ.

"faithful").[21] This negative description is intended to resonate with the audience in a particular way, reminding them of their pagan heritage and bringing to surface their duplicitous culture.[22] In this cultural and religious context, then, the adjective is subversive. The audience, who have been elected by this God, are called to be countercultural by exhibiting the sincerity of their conversion in their "godliness." That is, the audience are to embody a lifestyle of truth and godliness that is antithetical to the standard Cretan values of duplicity and greed.

Titus 1:2c (B'): Before Eternal Times

The phrase "before eternal (αἰωνίων) times" in the B' element (1:2c) echoes the phrase "on the basis of the hope of eternal (αἰωνίου) life" (1:2a) in the B element and so advances the audience's understanding of "eternal life." "Before eternal times" expresses to the audience the "transhistorical" framework for understanding God's promise to give "eternal life": the promise was conceived of before creation.[23] The audience, who have been promised "eternal life," understand better now what their future life will entail: they will transcend from a temporal existence to live with God in his "eternal time frame"—they will share in his "timelessness."[24] The prospect of participating in God's "timelessness" should draw the audience, as members of the "elect of God," to live lives qualitatively distinct from those around them who do not share in this hope.

The phrase also provides the framework for appreciating further the special place of Paul's apostolic ministry. God's divine plan to give life was hidden from human perception and understanding since it was conceived of "before eternal times." No person could possibly have known God's purposes through his own efforts. For this reason a representative—in this instance the apostle Paul—had to be sent in order to disclose God's eternal will.

In passing, it is worthwhile to note that the preposition "before" (πρό) reinforces for the audience its elect status (1:1a): prior to any action

---

21. See Collins, *Titus*, 306.

22. See Gray, "The Liar Paradox and the Letter to Titus," 302; Kidd, "Titus as Apologia," 185–209; Winter, *Roman Wives, Roman Widows*, 149–50.

23. See Towner, *Goal of Our Instruction*, 63–64; Barr, *Biblical Words for Time*, 75; Nielsen, "Scripture in the Pastoral Epistles," 4–23.

24. See Collins, *Titus*, 304.

on their part, God chose to give them life. The audience are reminded that they are recipients of grace. Therefore, their conduct in the present, which accords with their embrace of the truth, must be informed both by the future and the "past": they not only share in the "hope of eternal life" but are also driven by their experience of grace.

Titus 1:3–4 (A'): Titus, Paul's Genuine Son according to a Common Faith

In Titus 1:3–4 the audience hear the A' element of this unit (1:1–4) as a mini-chiasm in itself. Verses 3–4 are composed of three sub-elements:

a. ³ and revealed at the proper time (καιροῖς) his word in the proclamation with which I was considered faithful according to the command of God our savior (τοῦ σωτῆρος ἡμῶν θεοῦ)

  b. ⁴ᵃ To Titus, true child according to a common faith:

a'. ⁴ᵇ Grace (χάρις) and peace from God (θεοῦ) the Father and Christ Jesus our savior (σωτῆρος ἡμῶν).

The "a" (1:3) and "a'" (1:4b) sub-elements are parallel, given the assonances "time" (καιροῖς) and "grace" (χάρις) and the repetition of "God" (θεοῦ) and "our savior" (σωτῆρος ἡμῶν). The "b" sub-element (1:4a) is the only refrain in the A' element that refers to Titus, while the other sub-elements focus on God as the source of revelation and blessing.

Titus 1:3 (a): God's Word in Paul's Proclamation

In the "a" sub-element the audience are told that God "revealed at the proper time his word." Although the promise for "eternal life" was made "before eternal times," the apostle emphasizes that God has now "revealed" (ἐφανέρωσεν) it. The phrase "proper time" (καιροῖς ἰδίοις) refers to a "definite, fixed time"[25] and reminds the audience, the "elect of God" (1:1a), of God's sovereignty: God is moving according to his own will. In addition, the audience detect a development in God's eternal plan. They no longer live in an age of ignorance but in a period when the promise of eternal life has been revealed.

The audience also experience a shift in the object of the verbs from "eternal life" to "his word" (λόγον αὐτοῦ): instead of saying, "on the basis of eternal life that God promised . . . and revealed at the proper time," the apostle writes, "on the basis of eternal life that God promised

25. BDAG, s.v.

... and he revealed at the proper time his word." This anacoluthon draws the audience's attention from what is promised to the medium through which the promise is revealed and thus prepares them to appreciate further the import of Paul's gospel ministry.[26] Specifically, the audience hear that the "word" of God has been manifested now "in the proclamation" (ἐν κηρύγματι) of the apostle.[27] This "proclamation" is the "truth" (1:1b) concerning the promise of life that God has promised.

Paul adds the phrase, "with which I was considered faithful according to the command of God our savior." The audience learn three things. First, the passive form of the verb "considered faithful" reiterates that Paul's proclamation is not his own innovation but a message that has been given to him from God. Moreover, recalling the phrase "faith of the elect of God" (1:1a), the verb furthers the tie between Paul and the audience: Paul has been "considered faithful" (ἐπιστεύθην) to proclaim the word of God to deepen the faith (πίστιν) of the elect. Second, the pronoun "I" (ἐγώ) emphasizes that it is Paul who has been uniquely appointed to carry this message to the "elect of God," which includes the audience. Third, echoing the connotations of "slave of God and apostle of Jesus Christ" in 1:1a, the term "command" (ἐπιταγήν) highlights that Paul has authority because he is under authority. The audience understand, therefore, that they must submit to Paul's "proclamation" because it is ultimately God's "word" and because of the apostle's distinct and authoritative role in redemptive history.

The phrase "God our savior" (σωτῆρος ἡμῶν θεοῦ) not only introduces the important theme of salvation[28] but also expands the audience's understanding of who God is: the God whom Paul serves as a slave and the God of the elect (1:1a) has not only promised eternal life, but has also brought salvation. By referring to God as "our (ἡμῶν) savior," Paul reminds the audience of their participation with Paul and the "elect of God" in a saving and eternal relationship to God. The pronoun "our" thus serves to intensify the bond that the audience have with Paul.

---

26. See Towner, *Letters*, 672.

27. While "proclamation" (κηρύγματι) likely refers to the activity of preaching rather than the content, the distinction is sometimes blurred, as may be the case here.

28. For further discussion on the significance of the theme of salvation, see Malherbe, "'Christ Jesus Came into the World to Save Sinners,'" 331–38; Wieland, *The Significant of Salvations.*

Titus 1:4a (b): Titus, Paul's True Child

The audience have just heard Paul define his apostolic ministry in terms of God's great plan of salvation and the authoritative role he plays. In the "b" sub-element of the mini-chiasm, the apostle now extends his mission and authority to Titus.[29]

Paul addresses Titus as his "true child" (γνησίῳ τέκνῳ).[30] In the Hellenistic world familial connections were particularly important. The term "true" (γνησίῳ) implied "legitimate," referring to children born in wedlock.[31] The figurative application to Titus calls the audience to recognize Titus as Paul's legitimate representative.[32] Moreover, given the use of familial language, the audience perceive that Titus must do the will of his "father" even as Paul is obligated to do the will of his master. To facilitate Titus's own obedience the audience are to submit to Titus and support him in the fulfillment of the tasks that the apostle has given him. The qualifier "according to a common faith" defines even more precisely the nature of the relationship. That Titus shares in a "common faith (πίστιν)" as Paul, who was "considered faithful" (ἐπιστεύθην), communicates to the audience that Titus also has an authoritative and important role in furthering the "faith (πίστιν) of the elect of God" (1:1a).

Titus 1:4b (a'): Blessing of Grace and Peace

The accent on the divine initiative (καιροῖς) in the "a" sub-element continues in the greeting of "grace" (χάρις) in the "a'" sub-element. Paul's

29. The continuity between what Paul has said about himself and what he will say about and to Titus is indicated by the fact that the first four verses of the letter make up a single Greek sentence.

30. For NT occurrences of Titus, see 2 Cor 2:13; 7:6, 13, 14; 8:6, 16, 23; 12:18; Gal 2:1, 3; 2 Tim 4:10. What is apparent from these occurrences is that Titus was a trusted colleague of Paul who often served in a representative function. Specifically, Titus seemed to function as "Paul's crisis-intervention specialist"; see Witherington, *Letters*, 90. For more reflection on Titus as one of Paul's faithful co-workers, see Fellows, "Was Titus Timothy?" 33–58; Barrett, "Titus," 1–14; Johnson, *Letters*, 94–96; Ollrog, *Paulus und seine Mitarbeiter*, 23.

31. BDAG, s.v.

32. Some argue that the phrase "true child" indicates Titus was converted through Paul's ministry; see Collins, *Titus*, 308–18; Knight, *Pastoral Epistles*, 63–64; Witherington, *Letters*, 105. Others suggest Titus was ordained by Paul; see Joachim Jeremias, *Briefe an Timotheus und Titus*, 68–69. Verse 4a provides insufficient data to come to a conclusion. The point, however, is clear: Titus alone represents Paul legitimately to the Cretan believers.

first greeting expresses his desire for Titus and the audience, who have already been graced by their election and receipt of the promise of eternal life, to experience further "grace"—God's generous and freely given love.[33] This concept of the "grace" of God thus carries connotations of divine empowerment.[34] God's grace has elected the audience to become part of God's chosen people and will empower Titus and the Cretan community to live according to truth and godliness as the elect of God in Crete.

Along with "grace," Paul wishes "peace" (εἰρήνη), which expresses a sense of overall well-being.[35] The term indicates peace with God and peace between believers, which is possible through Christ Jesus. Paul's reference to "peace" reminds the audience not only of their new state with God but also of their calling to live at peace with one another and with the nonbelievers in Crete. Taken together with "grace," the two terms summarize for the audience the gospel: God's "grace" has been given to the elect through Christ and results in "peace."[36]

The terms "grace" and "peace" occur in non-epistolary Jewish liturgical contexts (see, e.g., Num 6:26; Ps 83:12). The form of the entire greeting suggests that it approximates a benediction or prayer that Paul may have given orally to a church.[37] Indeed, the absence of a verb in the greeting allows it to be heard in all three temporal dimensions: it affirms that the audience have received already "grace and peace" when they first heard the gospel; it indicates that the letter intends to give the audience a renewed experience of this "grace and peace" as they listen presently to the letter; and it prays that after, and as a result of, listening to the letter the audience may continue to experience and grow in "grace and peace."

In a development of the A element of the chiasm that mentions "God" in relation to "Paul, slave of God" and the "elect of God," and in a development of the "a" sub-element that mentions "God" as "savior,"

---

33. In the OT the term refers to the favoring love that God gives to his people; see Gen 6:8; 39:21; Exod 33:16. In the NT, and especially in Paul's gospel, God's gracious love has been given to his people through the life, death, and resurrection of Christ Jesus. "Grace," then, is a summary term for the gospel concerning Christ Jesus through which Paul, Titus, and the audience have become the "elect of God"; see Mounce, *Pastoral Epistles*, 10.

34. See Heil, *Ephesians*, 51; Harrison, *Paul's Language of Grace*, 243; Nolland, "Grace as Power," 26–31.

35. See Spicq, "εἰρενεύω," *TLNT* 1.424–38.

36. See Marshall, *Pastoral Epistles*, 134.

37. See Judith Lieu, "'Grace to You and Peace': The Apostolic Greeting," 167–78; Towner, *Letters*, 101.

in the A' element Paul designates "God" as "Father" (πατρός), alongside "Christ Jesus," as the source of "grace and peace." Despite ethnic, cultural, and socio-economic differences, Paul and the Cretan believers have one "Father" that has given all of them "grace and peace." In this sense, the term "Father" bonds the audience even more closely with Paul.

In the "a" sub-element the title of "savior" (σωτῆρος) is connected to "God." In the "a'" sub-element the application of the title to "Christ Jesus" communicates to the audience several points. First the designation of both the "Father" and "Christ Jesus" as "savior" links their distinct but related roles in the work of redemption. The former, according to 1:2, is the source of salvation, the latter is the means through which salvation is accomplished. Second, given the way the title was applied to various pagan gods, Roman emperors, and even model citizens, the pairing of "Christ Jesus" and "savior" was a subversive blow to the religious-political discourse of the time.[38] The Cretan believers are to recognize "Christ Jesus" alone as "savior." Third, the double reference to "savior" at the end of the "a" and "a'" sub-elements of this mini-chiasm and its strategic occurrence at the close of both this mini-chiasm and the first microchiasm prepare the audience to hear more of what Paul has to say about salvation and its ethical implications.

The reference to "Christ Jesus" (Χριστοῦ Ἰησοῦ) functions for the audience as the parallel between the A (1:1a) and the A' (1:4) elements of the first microchiasm. The order of the parallel is itself a mini-chiasm: Paul is an apostle of (a) Jesus (b) Christ in the A element, while grace and peace come from (b') Christ (a') Jesus in the A' element. Serving as the climax of the first chiastic unit, the phrase highlights how "Paul, apostle of Jesus Christ" (1:1a), "Titus, true child according to a common faith" (1:4), and the audience are united by grace and peace through Christ Jesus; hence, he is referred to as "our" savior. Thus, as Paul is called to represent Jesus Christ, so too the audience are to be "apostles" of Christ Jesus in Crete.

In the mini-chiasm of 1:3–4 the apostle cements three relationships—his relationship to "God our savior" (1:3), to Titus his "true child for a common faith" (1:4a), and to the Cretan believers who share in "grace and peace" (1:4b). In the first sub-element, the emphasis falls on Paul's proclamation that was given to him "by the command of God

---

38. See Witherington, *Letters*, 103–5; Towner, *Letters*, 676.

our savior." In the pivot, the emphasis falls on Titus's commitment to the apostle as his "true child." In the last sub-element, the emphasis falls on the unity between all believers as a result of their mutual experience of God's "grace" through Christ Jesus.

SUMMARY

1. Concerning the theme "Exhort and Reprove to Commendable Works according to the Hope of Eternal Life," Paul has introduced his audience in the first microchiastic unit to the theme that will develop in the remainder of the letter. Paul is a "slave of God and apostle of Jesus Christ" who has received from "God, who cannot lie," the proclamation concerning the "hope of eternal life" that was "promised before eternal times" and has now been "revealed." Commissioned "according to the faith of the elect of God," he seeks their "recognition of the truth that is according to godliness." Titus, who has been publicly recognized as the apostle's "true child according to a common faith," now possesses authority to continue the apostle's work. This work inevitably includes exhorting and reproving. As believers who share in "the hope of eternal life," the audience are to submit to Titus as an expression of their recognition of the unique role and authority that Paul has with respect to God's plan of salvation.

2. The first microchiasm (1:1–4) consists of five elements and introduces the theme "and Reprove to Commendable Works according to the Hope of Eternal Life."

3. In the opening elements of the chiasm (1:1–2a) Paul indicates that he has not only received the hope of eternal life by being appointed as a slave of God and apostle of Jesus Christ, but also responds to the hope of eternal life by exercising his apostleship in writing the letter to Titus and the audience members. The audience recognize that Paul's apostleship accords with their faith as members of the elect of God and, as coheirs of the hope of eternal life, are to respond to Paul's letter by paying careful attention to how it will deepen their recognition of the truth that is according to godliness.

4. As the audience hear the central element of the chiasm (1:2b), they realize that the God whom Paul serves is the God who cannot lie

and so stands diametrically opposed to both Zeus and their duplicitous culture. As members of the elect of God, the audience are to
pursue godliness by living countercultural lives in accordance with
the truth of the gospel. Since they possess the hope of eternal life,
the audience are to set themselves apart from the people of Crete.

5.   In the concluding element of the chiasm (1:3–4), Paul reiterates the
authority he has according to the command of God, and with that
authority he wishes continued grace and mercy to Titus and his
audience from God the Father and Christ Jesus our savior. This introductory prayer prepares the audience to receive and experience
more grace and peace by listening to the exhortation and reproof
that Christ will both communicate in the letter through his empowered apostle and effect through Titus.

4

Titus 1:5–13a: Exhort with Sound Doctrine and Reprove Opponents (B)

A. ⁵ *For this reason* I left you in *Crete*, so that what is left you might set right and appoint, according to city, elders, as I directed you, ⁶ if *one* is blameless, husband of one wife, having faithful children not in accusation of debauchery or *rebellious*. ⁷ For *it is necessary* that the overseer be blameless, as a *household-manager* of God, not arrogant, not irritable, not a drunkard, not belligerent, not *greedy for shameful gain*; ⁸ rather a lover-of-strangers, a lover-of-goodness, sensible, just, devout, self-controlled,

> B. ⁹ᵃ *holding fast* to the faithful *word* that is according to the *teaching*,
>
> B'. ⁹ᵇ so that he might be able both to exhort with sound *doctrine* and reprove *those who oppose*.

A'. ¹⁰ For there are many *rebels*, empty-talkers and deceivers, especially the circumcision, ¹¹ whom *it is necessary* to silence, who are upsetting whole *households*, teaching what *is not necessary* for this reason— shameful gain. ¹² *One* of them, their own prophet, said, "*Cretans* are always liars, evil beasts, lazy gluttons." ¹³ᵃ This testimony is true.[1]

AUDIENCE RESPONSE TO TITUS 1:5–13A

Titus 1:5–8 (A): Appoint Blameless Elders

I N TITUS 1:5–8 THE audience hear the A element of the second chiastic unit (1:5–13a) as a mini-chiasm in itself. Verses 5–8 are composed carefully of four sub-elements:

---

1. For the establishment of Titus 1:5–13a as a chiasm, see chapter 2.

a. [5] For this reason I left you in *Crete* (Κρήτῃ), so that what is left you might set right and appoint, according to city, elders, as I directed you,

b. [6] if one is *blameless* (ἀνέγκλητος), husband of one wife, having faithful children not in accusation of debauchery or rebellious.

b'. [7] For it is necessary that the overseer be *blameless* (ἀνέγκλητος), as a household-manager of God, not arrogant, not irritable, not a drunkard, not belligerent, not greedy for shameful gain;

a'. [8] rather a lover-of-strangers, a lover-of-goodness, sensible, just, devout, and *self-controlled* (ἐγκρατῆ),

Verses 5–8 form a cohesive unit centering on the appointment and qualities of "blameless" elders. While 1:9a-b adds another requirement, the shift in emphasis from characteristics (1:6–8) to calling (1:9a-b) distinguishes the A element from the B and B' elements.[2] The "a" (1:5) and "a" (1:8) sub-elements are parallel given the assonances "Crete" (Κρήτῃ) and "self-controlled" (ἐγκρατῆ).[3] The "b" (1:6) and "b'" sub-elements are also parallel given the repetition of "blameless" (ἀνέγκλητος). A movement is evident in the mini-chiasm, which begins with a focus on the elder's domestic life and then shifts to his public life.

Titus 1:5 (a): Appoint, according to City, Elders

Verse 1:5 strengthens Titus's authority, for Titus himself does not need to be reminded of why he was "left . . . in Crete." Rather, the audience need to recognize that Titus is "in Crete" according to the directive of Paul. The phrase "for this reason" (τούτου χάριν),[4] therefore, subtly reiterates that Titus ministers under and with the apostle's authority.

The verb "left" (ἀπέλιπόν) may allude to Paul's previous residence and ministry in Crete,[5] but within the context the emphasis falls less on Paul's departure and more on Titus's commission; thus, the sense of the verb is likely "dispatch."[6] The audience perceive that Paul "left" Titus in

2. Verses 1:9a-b are also grammatically distinguished from 1:7–8 through the use of the participle ἀντεχόμενον versus the repeated use of adjectives.

3. The parallelism is evident if one listens carefully to the twofold repetition of "κρ" and "τη/τῆ." Also, the adjective "self-controlled" (ἐγκρατῆ) is the next instance when the audience hear the sound "κρ" after 1:5.

4. In this instance τούτου is kataphoric, referring to what follows; see BDF §216.

5. See Mounce, *Pastoral Epistles*, 386.

6. See Johnson, *Letters*, 212; Jakob van Bruggen, *Die geschichtliche Einordnung der Pastoralbriefe*, 39–40; Wolter, *Die Pastoralbriefe als Paulustradition*, 186–90. This being

Crete for specific purposes, which is also implied by the conjunction "so that" (ἵνα). Moreover, they intuit that Titus's time with them is not indefinite. Rather, Titus has certain tasks to carry out and, upon completing them, will return to the apostle. From the outset, therefore, the audience sense a note of urgency: Titus's limited time with them signals the need to prepare for the vacuum of leadership that will follow with his departure.

Paul correlates artistically the action of leaving (ἀπέλιπον) Titus "in Crete" with the tasks of "what is left" (τὰ λείποντα) to do. The exact reference of the participle is unclear, referring either to unfinished work or the work of reformation. The preceding cognate verb suggests the former, that as Titus was "left in Crete" so too there is work left to complete. The proceeding verb "set right'" (ἐπιδιορθώσῃ) is a rare verb, absent in classical literature, the LXX, and the Fathers, but present in Cretan literature to express "reformation" with respect to laws and treaties.[7] For this reason the latter also seems plausible. It is probable that the apostle means to reflect two aspects of Titus's work through this dissonant construction: Titus is to complete unfinished work and bring reform where necessary.[8] The audience are thus oriented to the dual work of church leaders.

The conjunction καὶ, is epexegetical, expressing "particularly." Here Paul specifies for the audience the primary task that Titus is to carry out— "appoint, according to city, elders." The verb "appoint" (καταστήσῃς) denotes official appointments, i.e., appointments by Titus that are to be recognized and accepted by the audience.[9] The expression "according to city" (κατὰ πόλιν) reflects the organization of Crete into city-states during this time.[10] While it is difficult to determine the composition of

the case, Paul's familiarity with the Cretan culture in general (see 1:12), the level of intimacy when speaking about the audience (e.g., "Let *our* own also learn . . ." [4:14]), and his firsthand knowledge of the state of the churches in Crete, suggest that Paul did, in fact, minister in Crete for a period of time.

7. See Marshall, *Pastoral Epistles*, 151.

8. See Towner, *Letters*, 679.

9. The apostle does not mention how much of the responsibility is to be shared by the audience and how many elders are to be appointed. For various proposals, see Barrett, *The Pastoral Epistles*, 128–29; Knight, *Pastoral Epistles*, 288; Witherington, *Letters*, 107. What is clear is that Titus is to play a principal role in these appointments. Also, the closing clause in the sub-element, "as I directed you" (ὡς ἐγώ σοι διεταξάμην) indicates that Paul probably provided more details for Titus regarding the process.

10. Marshall, *Pastoral Epistles*, 152: "Crete was proverbial for its 'hundred' cities. . . . During classical and Hellenistic times about thirty-five city states are attested. This number was reduced to about twenty in the Roman period as some were taken over by more

a church in a given "city" (was there a single church or was the single church composed of smaller house congregations?), the prepositional phrase highlights further for the audience the extensiveness and thoroughness of the task given to Titus. "Elders" (πρεσβυτέρους) is a term that the early church inherited from Israel, referring not to "old men" but to the leaders of God's people.[11] The audience perceive that these men will serve as the extension of Paul and Titus's authority when Titus departs.

The clause at the end of the "a" sub-element, "as I directed you" reiterates for the audience that Titus is not working according to his own agenda and authority but according to the directive of the apostle; again, he has authority because he is under authority. In this sense, he is indeed Paul's "true child," because the apostle too does not lead according to his own authority but as a "slave of God and apostle of Jesus Christ" (1:1a). The personal pronoun "I" (ἐγώ) focuses the audience on Paul even though it is Titus who is tasked to carry out the work of appointing elders. The audience's support of Titus, then, is an acknowledgment of Paul's authority and ultimately the authority of God and Jesus Christ. The verb "directed" (διεταξάμην) carries both the sense of instruction and command.[12] The audience infer from this verb that Paul has provided explicit instructions to Titus already on how he is to carry out the work of appointing elders, including guidelines about the number of elders per city and the general process. In addition, the audience infer that Titus has been "considered faithful" with this task much in the way Paul was "considered faithful according to the command of God our savior" with the "word" (1:3).

Titus 1:6 (b): The Blameless Elder's Domestic Life

In the "b" sub-element the apostle begins listing the qualities of the elder. The syntax of 1:6 is a bit peculiar, although the sense is clear. It begins with the protasis of what appears to be a conditional statement: "if one is blameless." An apodosis, however, is missing. It is best, therefore, to read

---

powerful neighbors. Gortyna was the capital under Roman rule, but each city retained its own administration. They were notorious for their fierce rivalries, and only Roman jurisdiction ended the frequent inter-city wars."

11. See Exod 19:7; 2 Sam 3:17; Jer 36:1.

12. The verb "to command" (διατάσσω) appears four times in Paul's fiery letter to the Corinthians (1 Cor 7:17; 9:14; 11:34; 16:1). In each instance, the authority of the subject (whether Paul's or the Lord's) is highlighted. Therefore, while the verb implies the provision of detailed instructions, the nuance of authority is not to be missed.

this would-be protasis with the closing clause of 1:5 ("as I directed you") and then to understand what follows in 1:6 as an expansion of the term "blameless." F. F. Bruce's paraphrase expresses Paul's meaning well: "You remember those directions of mine about the kind of man who is fit to be appointed as an elder—one who is beyond reproach. . . ."[13]

Paul identifies "blameless" (ἀνέγκλητος) as the basic characteristic of the elder. The general background of the term is legal, underscoring the quality of being free from any charge in the domestic and civic domains.[14] The term highlights for the audience the need to choose leaders who will give no basis for accusation; in short, they are to adopt the highest of standards for the "one" (τίς) who aspires to this office.

Paul begins to elaborate on the term "blameless" by focusing the audience on the elder's family life. The first phrase indicates that the elder is to be the "husband of one wife" (μιᾶς γυναικὸς ἀνήρ). The audience hear the phrase as a reference to marital fidelity.[15] This conclusion is supported by the Greco-Roman concept of the *univira*, "one-husband woman."[16] The term denoted marital faithfulness in the Greco-Roman world and was given by husbands as an epithet to their deceased wives, as is evidenced in multiple tombstone inscriptions.[17] It is possible, therefore, that the stipulation in 1:6 of "one-wife husband" is patterned after this concept and that the audience hear echoes of the "one-husband wife." In addition, marital faithfulness was held in high esteem in the Greco-Roman world; thus, this quality would have commended the elder not only to church members but also to the surrounding pagans, a major concern for Paul.

The audience are told that the audience are also to have "faithful (πιστά) children." Prior to 1:6, the audience have heard the noun "faith" (πίστις) twice (1:1, 4), both of which pertain to faith in Jesus Christ. Given the proximity of 1:6 to 1:1 and 1:4, the audience likely hear "faithful children" as "believing children."[18] This interpretation is reiterated by

13. See Bruce, *The Letters of Paul*, 291.

14. MM §40.

15. For a brief but helpful summary of the various interpretations of the phrase, see Marshall, *Pastoral Epistles*, 155–57.

16. See Glasscock, "The Husband of One Wife," 244–58; Saucy, "Husband of One Wife," 229–40; Towner, *Goal of Our Instruction*, 232.

17. See Lightman and Zeisel, "Univira," 19–32.

18. For alternative interpretations, see Strauch, *Biblical Eldership*; Köstenberger, "Titus," 607.

the prepositional phrase that immediately follows. The phrase "not in accusation" (μὴ ἐν κατηγορίᾳ) expresses "not open to the charge of." The term "debauchery" (ἀσωτίας) indicates "wild living,"[19] which includes excessiveness with respect to spending, sexuality, eating, and drinking. Indeed, the phrase "not in accusation" echoes the term "blameless": like their fathers the children are not to be open to the charge of "wild living." The second term "rebellious" is a unique Hellenistic term that highlights insubordination. The alliteration "debauchery" (ἀσωτία) and "rebellious" (ἀνυπότακτος)[20] forms an apt description of the stereotypical Cretan. The audience, therefore, understand the children in view as believers who have set themselves apart from the Cretan world.

Thus the audience come to a deeper understanding between "recognition of the truth" and "godliness" (1:1b): the elder's recognition of truth should be reflected concretely in marital faithfulness and in the righteous upbringing of his children. For a first-century Greco-Roman culture that understands that an individual's good reputation depends on household solidarity, the requirements—though admittedly difficult—make sense. The audience perceive that the elder's ability to lead a church in Crete should be demonstrated first with his own household. Furthermore, Paul's concern for the leader's good reputation—based on the solidarity of his household—highlights for Titus and the Cretan community Paul's commitment to associate the gospel with men of repute. The first line of business for Titus and the Cretan community, then, is to identify this sort of "blameless" elder.

Titus 1:7 (b'): The Blameless Elder's Public Life from a "Negative" Perspective

Verse 7, the "b'" sub-element of the mini-chiasm, expands for the audience, by way of recall and reiteration of ἀνέγκλητον in the "b" sub-element, the meaning of "blameless" (ἀνέγκλητον). The conjunction "for" (γάρ) indicates the connection between 1:6 and 1:7. There are, however, a few changes that point to a progression from the domain of the household to the public sphere. First, although the repetition of "blameless" and the context make it clear that the office of elder is still in view, Paul uses the

---

19. BDAG, s.v.

20. This is the precise term used later to describe the rebellious teachers in the community (1:10).

different term "overseer" (ἐπίσκοπον) in 1:7.[21] The two terms bring out different emphases of the same office. "Elders" (πρεσβυτέρους) focuses more on "being"—*who* the person is. "Overseer" (ἐπίσκοπον) underscores the elder's function as guardian: the emphasis is not so much on *who* he is but *what* he does. In short, the two terms capture "the form and function" of the single position and are to be understood as synonyms.[22]

The progression from 1:6 to 1:7 is also borne out by the phrase "household-manager of God" (θεοῦ οἰκονόμον). While Paul focused initially on the elder candidate's ability to manage his own household well, now the focus shifts to the oversight of God's household. In Greek literature, the term οἰκονόμον often refers to an entrusted manager of a household or estate.[23] The status and duties of a "household-manager of *God* (θεοῦ)," then, are comparable to Paul's calling as a "slave of *God* (θεοῦ)" (1:1a): both have representative authority and are held accountable only to their masters. The similarities between the two positions communicate clearly to the audience the relationship between Paul and the future elders. For the time being Titus serves as Paul's authorized representative among the churches in Crete. His time with the Cretans, however, will come to an end after he completes the tasks that the apostle has given him. At that time the elders will take up the leadership of God's household, i.e., the churches in Crete. The audience's recognition of Paul and Titus's authority must be transferred eventually to the elders who serve on the same trajectory as the two. The household imagery also challenges the audience to see the churches as families and members as fathers, mothers, brothers, and sisters. Within this perspective they recognize that the elder plays a pivotal role in a church comparable to that of the father in a household.

In Titus 1:7–8, the last two sub-elements of the mini-chiasm, the apostle elaborates on what it means for the elder to be "blameless" by providing two lists of contrasting characteristics. In the first he details what the elder must *not* be; in the second what the elder *must* be. The

---

21. For an extended discussion of overseers and their relation to elders, see Marshall, *Pastoral Epistles*, 170–81; Merkle, *The Elder and Oversee*; Young, "On Episkopos and Presbyteros," 142–48.

22. See Marshall, *Pastoral Epistles*, 177. Cf. Campbell, *The Elders*, Bassler, *Titus*, 186; Fee, *Titus*, 174; Mounce, *Pastoral Epistles*, 221; Harvey, "Elders," 330–31.

23. Spicq, "οἰκονόμος," *TLNT*, 2. 568–75; Reumann, "'Stewards of God," 339–40; Marshall, *Pastoral Epistles*, 160.

lists here are not meant to be complete, and yet—taken together—they portray holistically what the blameless elder should look like.

The apostle begins the first list with the repetition of "not" (μή) in the list of negative attributes, enabling the audience to recall the comprehensive significance of the term "blameless." "Blameless" means "*not* arrogant," "*not* irritable," "*not* a drunkard," "*not* belligerent," and "*not* greedy for shameful gain."

First, "it is necessary" that the "overseer" is not "arrogant" (αὐθάδης). The vice is expressed concretely as stubbornness—a refusal to heed the advice and warnings of others stemming from a mixture of pride and uncontrollable anger (e.g., Gen 49:3; Prov 21:24). Second, the elder must not be "irritable" (ὀργίλος), i.e., "inclined to anger" or "quick-tempered."[24] Third, he must not be addicted to wine, for a "drunkard" (pa,roinoj) tends to act foolishly because he has lost his ability to discern right from wrong. Fourth, he must not be "belligerent" (πλήκτης). That this vice follows "drunkard" suggests an association between the two.[25] In addition, the emphasis on nonviolence contrasts the violent tendencies of Cretans who were engaged regularly in intercity wars and piracy.[26] Finally, the elder must not be "greedy for shameful gain" (αἰσχροκερδής). For the audience this final vice resonates deeply, for Cretans were known for their greed.[27]

The elder, then, represents the Cretan antitype, an individual who has shed the Cretan values and taken on "godliness" out of "recognition of the truth" (1:1b). Those among the audience who are aspiring to be elders feel the force of this first list and are sobered by the high standard that the apostle has given: the elder is the Cretan antitype. The audience, however, have heard only half of the qualities necessary to be the "blameless" elder. The repetition of the negative particle mh, has prepared them to ask positively, "What, then, must the elder be?"

The mini-chiasm comes to a climactic conclusion in 1:8, the "a'" subelement. The absence of vice alone, for Paul, does not qualify an individual to become the elder; "rather" (ἀλλά) the elder must exhibit also virtues.

---

24. BDAG, s.v.

25. See Quinn, *Letter*, 80; Roland Schwarz, *Bürgerliches Christentum im Neuen Testament*, 54.

26. See Marshall, *Pastoral Epistles*, 202.

27. See Polybius *Histories* 6.45–46.

First, "it is necessary"[28] for the elder to be a "lover-of-strangers" (φιλόξενον), i.e., "hospitable."[29] The quality has in view hospitality to Christian refugees[30] and the practical need for homes that would serve as meeting places for worship.[31] The prefix φιλ- indicates that the elder must have a special interest in or affinity for these matters.[32] Second, the elder must be a "lover-of-goodness" (φιλάγαθον). In the Pauline epistles, the adjective "good" (ἀγαθός) refers often to "things characterized especially in terms of social significance and worth."[33] Third, the elder must be "sensible" (σώφρονα). The term describes one who avoids extremes, who is moderate in lifestyle so as not to be tempted by bribes and who gives careful consideration for responsible action.[34] The revelation of the plan of salvation (1:2–3) provides for the audience the new framework for determining what is excessive, beneficial, and wise.[35] Fourth, the elder must be "just" (δίκαιον). In the Greco-Roman tradition, this adjective describes one who is committed to upholding "natural law" by doing what is right and fair, which results in a healthy and stable society. Paul's use of the term, however, includes a godward reference. Fifth, the elder must be "devout" (ὅσιον). For the audience the term expresses devotion—outward purity reflecting an inward piety. Finally, the elder must be "self-controlled" (ἐγκρατῆ). Held as a cardinal virtue among Greek writers, the term connotes discipline over fleshly impulses and desires. This last virtue is related to the third virtue "sensible."[36] The former, however, focuses on sober thinking, the latter on checking bodily desires. The adjective "self-controlled" (ἐγκρατῆ) in the a' sub-element is in assonance with "Crete" (Κρήτη) in 1:5 of the a sub-element. It reminds the audience that Cretans are indulgent people, embodying the antithesis of a

---

28. The force of the verbs δεῖ . . . εἶναι continues in 1:8.

29. BDAG, s.v.

30. See Quinn, *Letter*, 90–91.

31. See Marshall, *Pastoral Epistles*, 163.

32. See φιλέω in BDAG.

33. BDAG, s.v.

34. BDAG, s.v.

35. For further comments on the relationship between "sensible" and the promise of eternal life, see Marshall, *Pastoral Epistles*, 182–84. Here Marshall highlights how the "Christ-event" has changed radically the original meaning of σώφρων.

36. For a discussion of σώφρων and related concepts, see Marshall, *Pastoral Epistles*, 182–91.

"self-controlled" life. That the elder, then, is to be the Cretan anti-type is reiterated for the audience in the last adjective of the closing sub-element.

Titus 1:9a (B): Elders Who Hold Fast to the Faithful Word

Verse 9a, the B element of the second microchiastic unit, begins the final qualification of the elder: "holding fast to the faithful word that is according to the teaching." The shift from simple adjectives (1:7–8) to a participle (1:9a–b) signals for the audience the special importance of this last qualification.

The verb "holding fast" (ἀντεχόμενον) occurs throughout the OT in different literary genres (e.g., Neh 4:10; Prov 3:18; Jer 2:8). The sense of standing one's ground in the face of hostile opposition is borne out particularly in 1 Macc 15:25–36, which recounts Antiochus VII's threat against Simon. Simon's response is: "Now that we have the opportunity, we are holding fast (ἀντεχόμεθα) to the heritage of our ancestors" (15:34). For Titus and the Cretan community, therefore, the verb invokes images of standing staunchly—in an almost militant way—against those who would try to lead them away from the "word" (1:3) that has been given to them by Paul. The verb also implies for the audience the presence of opposition that threatens faithfulness to the word of God.

The object of the verb is "the faithful word that is according to the teaching" (τοῦ κατὰ τὴν διδαχὴν πιστοῦ λόγου). The audience heard the term "word" (λόγον) in 1:3 as that which "God, who cannot lie," (1:2b) "revealed at the proper time" (1:3). For this reason it is inherently a "trustworthy" or "believable" "word." In 1:9a the "word" (λόγου) is qualified as "faithful" (πιστοῦ). The audience members were just informed that the elder must have "faithful (πιστά) children" (1:6), i.e., "believing" children. Maintaining both nuances, then, the phrase "faithful word" communicates to the audience that the word is the believable word held by believers.[37]

The "word" is also qualified by the phrase "according to the teaching." In the context of the letter, "teaching" (διδαχήν) is equivalent to Paul's "proclamation, which includes the gospel and doctrines of which the apostle instructed them already.[38] Only teaching and preaching that accord with what the apostle himself proclaimed are to be accepted by

---

37. See Quinn, *Letters to Titus*, 92.

38. See Marshall, *Pastoral Epistles*, 166; Towner, *Letters*, 692.

the audience as the "faithful word." The piling on of modifiers for the "word"—to the point of almost redundancy—communicates to the audience that in the apostle's estimation there is only one authoritative "word" which they, under the leadership of the leaders, must hold fast to.

3. Titus 1:9b (B'): Elders Who Are Able Both to Exhort and Reprove

Following the requirement of "holding fast" to the "faithful word" in the B element, the apostle gives the twofold (καί . . . καί) ministerial purpose (i[να) of the requirement in the B' element (1:9b): "so that he might be able both to exhort with sound doctrine and reprove those who oppose." At this point, the audience hear a pivot in the chiastic parallels from "holding fast" (ἀντεχόμενον) and "teaching" (διδαχήν) in the B element to "those who oppose" (ἀντιλέγοντα) and "doctrine" (διδασκαλία) in the B' element. The clause so that he "might *be able*" (δυνατὸς ᾖ) indicates that the elder's ability to exhort and reprove depends directly on his commitment to the "faithful word." That such an individual becomes "able" to carry out the work of the elder is highlighted by the repetition of καί: such an elder is "able *both* to exhort . . . and reprove"; in short, he is equipped fully to carry out his work if he holds firmly to the "word." In a subtle way Paul elevates further the status that the "word" should have among the Cretan believers.

By "holding fast" to the "faithful word," the elder is able "to exhort with sound doctrine." The verb "to exhort" (παρακαλεῖν) can mean "to encourage," but the incipient state of the churches, which is implied by the absence of elders, and emphasis in the introduction on godliness lend toward interpreting the verb to mean "to exhort"—to give "practical authoritative teaching that compels believers to implement the faith in all aspects of life."[39] In Greco-Roman literature, the term "sound" (ὑγιαινούσῃ) often expressed good health."[40] Therefore, the phrase "sound *doctrine*" communicates to the audience doctrine that will make the churches healthy. The similarity in sound between "doctrine" (διδασκαλία) in the B' element and "teaching" (διδαχήν) in the B element suggests they are to be understood as synonyms. The very "word," then, that is "according to the teaching" is also the "word" that brings health to the believing community. The elder must exhort with this "faithful word" that enriches the

39. Towner, *Letters*, 692.
40. BDAG, s.v.

faith of the elect even as Paul himself currently writes "sound doctrine" for their edification.

In addition, by "holding fast" to the "faithful word," the elder is "able to . . . reprove those who oppose." The object "those who oppose" (ἀντιλέγοντας) comes before "reprove" in the Greek text. This sequence focuses the audience's attention on this group whose identity remains somewhat vague. In the OT, while the verb ἀντιλέγω carries occasionally the plain meaning of responding to a statement or question, in many instances it connotes disobedience and rebellion (e.g., Isa 65:2; Esth 8:8). In addition, the B-B' parallelism offers some insight into the identity of the group. On the one hand, the elder "holds fast" (ἀντεχόμενον) to the "word" (λόγου), the very "word" (λόγον) that God "revealed" in Paul's "proclamation" (1:3) and so is "faithful" and "sound." On the other hand, the antithetical group are "those who oppose" (ἀντιλέγοντας). The assonances lead the audience to interpret the two groups in light of each other. They conclude that the former are for the "word," the latter against it; the former "hold fast" to it, the latter reject it.

The verb "to reprove" (ἐλέγχω) is common in the OT, connoting a strong sense of correction bordering on condemnation and punishment is in view (e.g., Gen 21:25; Ps 6:1; Isa 2:4). Thus, while the verb may include a sense of correcting false doctrine,[41] the audience perceive that it includes also a sense of correcting bad behavior.[42] The present tense of the participle ἀντιλέγοντας suggests to the audience that this group is a real and present danger. It suggests that their activities have not abated but persist and threaten the vitality of the Cretan churches. Therefore, the audience appreciate the urgency behind the reiteration to appoint elders who will "reprove" "those who oppose" and recognize the need to help Titus carry out this difficult and extensive task.

Titus 1:10–13a (A'): The Rebellious False Teachers

In Titus 1:10–13a the audience hear the A' element of the second chiastic unit (1:5–13a) as a mini-chiasm in itself. Verses 10–13a are composed carefully of four sub-elements:

---

41. BDAG, s.v.

42. For this reason I have translated ἐλέγχειν as "reprove" instead of "refute" (NAB) or "rebuke" (ESV). "Refute" seems to focus on correcting false doctrine, "rebuke" on bad behavior. "Reprove" captures both dimensions.

a. ¹⁰ For there *are* (εἰσίν) many rebels, empty-talkers and deceivers, especially the circumcision

    b. ¹¹ᵃ whom *it is necessary* (δεῖ) to silence, who are upsetting whole households,

    b′. ¹¹ᵇ teaching what is not *necessary* (δεῖ) for this reason—shameful gain.

  a′. ¹² One of them, their own prophet, said, "Cretans are always liars, evil beasts, lazy gluttons." ¹³ᵃ This testimony *is* (ἐστίν) true.

The mini-chiasm exhibits a clear movement: Paul's open reproof of "those who oppose" climaxes in the affirmation of the "testimony" that "Cretans are always liars, evil beasts, lazy gluttons": they are the epitome of every notorious Cretan vice. The mini-chiasm runs parallel to the A element and so instructs the audience to recognize how these "rebels" stand in marked contrast to Paul, Titus, and the elder.

Verses 10–13a form a cohesive unit, expanding on the identity of "those who oppose" "sound doctrine." The cognates of "to be" (εἰμί)— "For there are (εἰσίν) many rebels" in the "a" sub-element and "This testimony is (ἐστίν) true" in the "a′" sub-element—form an *inclusio*. These are the only occurrences of the verb "to be" in this mini-chiasm. They surround the "b" and "b′" sub-elements which are held together by the common verb δεῖ, establishing the parallelism of the central elements in the second mini-chiasm. These are the only occurrences of the verb "it is necessary" in the mini-chiasm.

Titus 1:10 (a)

That the A′ element is to be heard in light of what Paul just stated in 1:9b concerning the elder who is able to exhort and reprove is indicated by the conjunction "for" (γάρ). The present tense of the verb "there are" (εἰσίν) reiterates for the audience that Paul is addressing a present and serious problem. The urgency of the situation is accentuated further by the term "many" (πολλοί).

In the "a" sub-element Paul reproves "those who oppose" in three ways: they are "rebels" (ἀνυπότακτοι), "empty-talkers" (ματαιολόγοι) and "deceivers" (φρεναπάται). Each of these descriptions has been chosen carefully by the apostle. First, recalling that the "blameless" elder must have "faithful children not in accusation of debauchery or rebellious (ἀνυπότακτα)" (1:6), the audience perceive that one of the trademarks of this opposing group is their flagrant disregard for legitimate authority. Like rebellious children who reject parental authority that God has established, this group does not honor the apostolic authority that God has established through Paul. This descriptor suggests also that "those who oppose" will rebel against the future elders as well.

Second, these opponents are "empty-talkers" (ματαιολόγοι). The adjective μάταιος expresses "empty."[43] Having heard how the apostle describes the "word," the audience recognize the import of the prefix to ματαιολόγοι. The "word" that the elder must cling to is the "faithful word" (πιστοῦ λόγου, 1:9a) because it is the "word" (λόγον) of God that has been "revealed" in the apostle's "proclamation" (1:3). Because this "word" is from "God, who cannot lie" (1:2b), it is trustworthy and grants health to the church. In short, this "word" is the "full and meaningful" word. Therefore, the term "empty-talkers" (ματαιολόγοι) is more than a possible reference to gossip; rather it denounces both the teachers and the teaching of "those who oppose" truth. Their "word"—in contrast to the "word" of God to which the elders hold fast—is empty and meaningless.[44]

Third, these opponents are "deceivers" (φρεναπάται). The descriptor is likely focusing on the opponents' teaching and is a fitting final characterization. Recognizing the verb "to walk" (πατέω) in the term "deceivers" (φρεναπάται), the audience perceive that such individuals are false guides for learning how to "walk" according to "sound doctrine" (1:9a). By denouncing these opponents as false guides, the apostle widens the gap between them and the elders who will "exhort with sound doctrine." In doing so, the doctrinal and ethical import of choosing sides becomes increasingly clear to the audience. They recognize the presence of two antithetical groups and must therefore choose which group they will ultimately follow.

The apostle specifies the identity of these "rebels, empty-talkers and deceivers" in the closing prepositional phrase of the first sub-element: "especially the circumcision." The adverb "especially" (μάλιστα) points out for the audience that among the "many" (πολλοί) most come from "the circumcision." The specific reference to "circumcision" signals for the

---

43. BDAG, s.v.

44. Towner, *Letters*, 695: "The comparison made in this way . . . was between truth and error, and far more was at stake than simply wasting time." See also *Schlarb, Die gesunde Lehre*, 59–73.

audience the particular "Judaizing" practice and the related beliefs that characterize the opponents. While the apostle does not detail the content of what these opponents teach, in some general sense it is related to Jewish beliefs and practices that run counter to the "word."

Titus 1:11a (b)

Paul now exhorts Titus and the Cretan community to reprove these opponents because of their impact on other believers: "whom it is necessary to silence, who are upsetting whole households." The verb "it is necessary" (δεῖ) in the A' element echoes its first occurrence in the A element where the apostle stated that "it is necessary (δεῖ) that the overseer be blameless" (1:7). The repetition of the adjective "blameless" in 1:6 and 1:7 highlights that blamelessness is an absolute must for the elder. Similarly, the audience understand the exhortation to "silence" the opposition as an absolute must; each is as necessary as the other. The verb "silence" (ἐπιστομίζειν) contains the term "mouth" (στόμα) and points out for the audience the source of the problem with the opponents—their mouths, i.e., their teaching. The translation "silence" is benign compared to the more literal translation "put something on the mouth"—to gag.[45] By using such forceful language, the apostle highlights further for the audience the urgency of the situation and the extreme measures that must be taken. The audience, in turn, perceive that it is primarily the exhortation and reproof of the elders that will "gag" these mouths.

These opponents pose a threat to the church because they are "upsetting whole households." Again, the contrast with elders is highlighted for the audience. While the elder is the "husband of one wife, having faithful children" (1:6), in short, a man who upholds his household, these opponents "upset whole households." The extent of their destructive influence is highlighted by the adjective "whole" (ὅλους). The verb "upsetting" (ἀνατρέπουσιν) contains the verb τρέπω, which means "to turn."[46] While it expresses figuratively "upsetting" or "overturning," more literally it indicates that the opponents are turning "whole households" away from the "word." The term "households" (οἴκους) likely refers to places where local churches met for worship[47] and recalls for the audience the descrip-

45. BDAG, s.v.

46. BDAG, s.v.

47. For more information on house churches as places of worship, see White, "Social Authority," 209–28; Linton, "House Church Meetings," 229–44; Craffert, "The Pauline Household Communities," 309–41.

tor "household-manager" (οἰκονόμον) in 1:7 of the A element. These opponents embody the antithesis of the elder given they are tearing down rather than building up the "faith of the elect of God" (1:1a).

Titus 1:11b (b')

In the "b'" sub-element the apostle indicates how the opponents are "upsetting whole households" and what their motivation is: "teaching what is not necessary for this reason— shameful gain." The verb "silence" in the "b" sub-element highlights the source of the problem—the "mouths" of the opponents, i.e., their teaching. This reference is made explicit in the "b'" sub-element through the participle "teaching" (διδάσκοντες). The use of the participle contrasts again the opponents and elders: while the elder must "hold fast to the faithful word that is according to the teaching (διδαχήν) so that he might be able . . . to exhort with sound doctrine (διδασκαλίᾳ)" (1:9a-b), these opponents are upsetting the faith of many by "teaching (διδάσκοντες) what is not necessary," i.e., what contradicts the "teaching" and "sound doctrine."[48] The present tense of "teaching" suggests that these opponents are recognized even now as teachers by more than a few among the audience.[49] The third occurrence of the verb "it is necessary" (δεῖ) reflects Paul's rhetorical strategy in the A-A' parallels of this second microchiasm: "it is necessary" for the elder to be blameless and to hold fast to sound doctrine in order to reprove those for whom "it is necessary" to silence (1:11a) because they are teaching what "is not necessary" (1:11b).

To discredit the opponents further, the apostle yet again contrasts the opponents with the elders in the last phrase of 1:11b: "for this reason—shameful gain." The assertion reiterates that these opponents represent the antithesis of the elder who, according to the A element, must not be "greedy for shameful gain" (αἰσχροκερδῆ). The preposition "for this reason" (χάριν) echoes its first occurrence in the A element where Paul states, "For this reason (χάριν) I left you in Crete" (1:5) and then proceeds to outline the explicit purpose for which Titus is in Create. Recalling this earlier use, the audience perceive that the opponents teach

48. Marshall adds, "As in 1 Tim 1.7, the indefinite reference to the doctrines of the opponents is pejorative and stands in vivid contrast to the descriptions of the apostolic teaching as τοῦ κατὰ τὴν διδαχὴν πιστοῦ λόγου and τῇ διδασκαλίᾳ τῇ ὑγιαινούσῃ in v. 9" (*Pastoral Epistles*, 197).

49. See Towner, *Letters*, 697.

for this express purpose—"shameful gain." Knowing that "shameful gain" is *the* Cretan vice, especially among sophists who were driven by money, the audience recognize that the closing phrase associates the opponents with the worst vice of Cretan society.

Titus 1:12–13a (a')

In this last sub-element, Paul concludes both the mini-chiasm and the second chiastic unit with a quote from "one of them, their own prophet."[50] The vague preface, "One (τις) of them," may reflect Paul's disdain and disregard for "them" (αὐτῶν).[51] The expression, "their own prophet," does not mean that the apostle views the "prophet" (προφήτης) as having the same authority and status as OT prophets. Rather, the designation reflects both his knowledge of how Cretans would describe their great teachers and poets and the apostle's ability to use the traditions available to him for his own historical and rhetorical purposes.[52]

The repetition of the pronoun (αὐτῶν) creates distance between the audience and the Cretan prophet: "One *of them, their* own prophet." The first occurrence of "one" (τις) in 1:6 of the A element refers to "one" among the audience who can serve as the elder; in 1:12 it refers to "one" among Cretan unbelievers. Having established the unity between Paul and the audience through the twofold use of the pronoun "our" (ἡμῶν) in 1:3 and 1:4 of the first microchiasm, Paul challenges the audience now through the twofold use of the pronoun αὐτῶν to distance themselves from their surrounding pagan culture: this "prophet" is "one of *them, their* own prophet," not "one" from the audience like the "apostle of Jesus Christ" (1:1a); thus the audience are not to esteem this Cretan prophet. While such "prophets" occasionally speak truths, for the audience truth comes ultimately from "God, who cannot lie" (1:2b) and who has "revealed at the proper time his word" in Paul's "proclamation" (1:3). The audience recognize, therefore, that while the apostle is about to quote from the Cretan prophet, he does not revere the individual; he is bordering on

---

50. Traditionally, this saying is attributed to Epimenides, a religious teacher and miracle performer who lived about 600 BC. Still the actual origin is uncertain, some speculating that it should be attributed to Callimachus. See Kidd, "Titus," 188–93; Mounce, *Pastoral Epistles*, 398–99; Winter, *Roman Wives*, 151.

51. For this pejorative use of τις, see Towner, *Letters*, 108, 699.

52. See Towner, *Letters*, 700.

sarcasm to make the point that even "their own" (referring to "those who oppose") condemn them.

The preface of the quote has one additional ironic point: although the opponents are "the circumcision" (1:10), the prefatory phrases associate these Jewish opponents with the Cretan prophet. The implication is that the two belong together even though they are ethnically different, whereas the audience now belong to the "elect of God" (1:1a) with Paul even though they are ethnically different. The audience are implicitly taught to view all people differently in light of the common grace and peace they have received (1:4). This point progresses the earlier observation that the audience are to adopt a new perspective concerning the constituents of God's household; kinship is based less on ethnicity and more on faith, as Paul demonstrated in his reference to Titus as "true child according to a common faith" (1:4).

The quote contains three parts that attack the speech and behavior of the opponents: "Cretans are always liars, evil beasts, lazy gluttons." The crux of the criticism lies with the adverb "always" (ἀεί) which connotes "from time immemorial."[53] The indictment that follows has been true for Cretans through the ages. The adverb sounds much like the promise of "eternal life" that God "promised before eternal (αἰωνίων) times" (1:2b–c). The apostle states implicitly that the audience can rely on Cretans for their immorality just as they can rely on God for his faithfulness to give "eternal (αἰωνίου) life" (1:2a).

As "liars" (ψεῦσται) Cretans stand in stark contrast to the "God, who cannot lie (ἀψευδής)" (1:2):[54] as truthfulness is part of God's essence, duplicity is part of Cretan existence. The second part of the quote is surprising, given that Crete was known for its lack of wild animals.[55] The term "beasts" (θηρία) is applied figuratively to describe wicked people, and, taken with the adjective "evil" (κακά), which could be translated "harmful,"[56] it highlights the destructive impact of the opponents. Reggie

---

53. Marshall, *Pastoral Epistles*, 201.

54. The phrase "Cretans are always liars" is found verbatim in Callimachus *Hymn to Zeus* 8. Callimachus includes the explanation for this indictment: "Yes, a tomb, O Lord, for you the Cretans built; but you did not die, for you are eternal" (8–9).

55. See Towner, *Letters*, 701.

56. BDAG, s.v.

M. Kidd captures the point of this expression well: "Crete had no need of wild beasts, for its own inhabitants were sufficient."[57]

The last part of the quote is also surprising, given that Cretans were active in warfare, piracy, and the like.[58] Here, the opponents are active in "teaching." The adjective "lazy" is to be understood with respect to "good works," i.e., works which edify the community. The term "gluttons" (γαστέρες), which means "bellies" literally, communicates to the audience the absence of self-control. By "teaching what is not necessary for this reason—shameful gain," the opponents prove that their bellies are insatiable—that they are willing to do anything for gain. The entire phrase was a common slur in antiquity to describe the individual who loved to eat without working for his food.[59] Here the apostle uses the phrase to describe the false teachers who seek to prosper from the churches without contributing anything beneficial.

Paul concludes the mini-chiasm and the second microchiasm in 1:13a with the declaration, "This testimony is true." "Testimony" (μαρτυρία) means "attestation of character or behavior,"[60] and the testimony in view is "this" (αὕτη), i.e., the saying from "their own prophet." The adjective "true" (ἀληθής) echoes the noun "truth" (ἀληθείας) in 1:1b of the first microchiasm, which was understood by the audience as an expression of "things as they really are." The "truth" that the audience have received is Paul's gospel-proclamation, which has at its center the unlying God. Within this gospel-framework "this testimony" concerning the Cretans is all the more "true."[61]

SUMMARY OF CHAPTER FOUR

1. The theme "Exhort and Reprove to Commendable Works according to the Hope of Eternal Life" becomes more explicit in the second microchiasm. According to the first element Paul left Titus in Crete (1:5) to appoint men who are "blameless" in both their pri-

---

57. Kidd, "Titus," 190.

58. Ibid., 191.

59. Witherington, *Letters*, 124.

60. BDAG, s.v.

61. This interpretation of the meaning and application of 1:12–13a is more straightforward than complicated theories related to the so-called "liar's paradox"; see Gray, "Liar Paradox," 302–14; Thiselton, "Logical Role," 207–23.

vate (1:6) and public lives (1:7–8). The "blameless" elder is not only to lack negative qualities (1:7) but also to exhibit positive qualities (1:8). According to the B and B' elements, which form the pivot of the microchiasm, the elder candidate must "hold fast to the faithful word that is according to the teaching" for the explicit twofold purpose of exhorting with sound doctrine and reproving opponents (1:9a-b). In the A' element Paul describes the group that stands in opposition to the "blameless" elder, Paul, and Titus. "It is necessary to silence" (1:11) these "rebels," especially because their greedy motives and false teaching are "upsetting whole households."

2. The second microchiasm (1:5–13a) consists of four elements and progresses the theme "Exhort and Reprove to Commendable Works according to the Hope of Eternal Life."

3. In the opening element of the chiasm (1:5–8), Paul makes explicit his reason for leaving Titus in Crete and provides a list of qualities concerning the "blameless" elder for the audience members. By doing so Paul continues to exercise his apostleship in writing the letter to Titus and the Cretan community members. In recognition of Paul's apostolic exhortation ("as I directed you," 1:5), the audience are to respond by discerning men who display these qualities, which should be evident in all who belong to the "elect of God" (1:1a), and who demonstrate their "recognition of the truth according to godliness" (1:1b).

4. As the audience hear the central elements of the chiasm (1:9a-b), they perceive the special emphasis that the apostle places on the elder's commitment to "hold fast" to the "faithful word." Only by doing so can the elder "exhort with sound doctrine and reprove those who oppose." Again, in recognition of Paul's apostleship the audience are to pursue men who will exhort and reprove according to the "word" that was revealed in Paul's "proclamation" (1:3). In addition, cognizant now of "those who oppose" the "faithful word," the audience must aid Titus in the urgent task of appointing elders "according to city" (1:5).

5. In the concluding element of the chiasm (1:10–13a), Paul specifies the identity of "those who oppose," exhorts the audience to reprove them (1:10), and condemns these rebels as the embodiment of

Cretan depravity. Possessing this knowledge, the audience must be wary of their teaching and curb their influence by silencing them lest they wreak more havoc. Moreover, the contrast between "those who oppose" and the "blameless" elders challenges the audience to shift their allegiance from those who are "teaching what is not necessary" (1:11) to those who are "holding fast to the faithful word that is according to the teaching" (1:9a).

5

Titus 1:13B—3:3: Reprove and Exhort with Sound Doctrine as We Await Our Savior (B')

A. [13b] Therefore, *reprove* them severely, so that they might be sound in the faith, [14] not paying attention to Jewish myths and commands of *human beings* who turn away the truth. [15] All things are clean to the clean. But to the defiled and unfaithful nothing is clean; rather, defiled are both their mind and conscience. [16] God they profess to know but by their works they deny, being vile and *disobedient* and unqualified *for all good work.*

> B. [2:1] But you *speak* what is consistent with sound doctrine. [2] Older men are to be temperate, serious, sensible, sound in faith, in love, in endurance. [3] Older women, similarly, are to be reverent in behavior, not slanderers, not enslaved to much wine, commendable teachers [4] so that they may make sensible the younger women to be lovers-of-husbands, lovers-of-children, [5] sensible, chaste, homemakers, good, submitting to their own husbands, so that the word of God might not be blasphemed. [6] *Exhort* the younger men to be similarly sensible [7] about all things, presenting yourself as a model of *commendable works,* in the doctrine incorruption, seriousness, [8] sound word that is beyond reproach, so that the opponent may be put to shame, having nothing bad to say about us. [9] Slaves are to submit to their own masters in all things, to be pleasing, not those who oppose, [10a] not those who pilfer; rather those who demonstrate that all faith is good,

> > C. [10b] so that they might adorn the doctrine of God our *savior* in all things. [11] For the grace of God has *appeared, saving* all human beings, [12] training us, so that by denying ungodliness

and worldly desires we may live sensibly and righteously and godly in the present age,

D. ^{13a} awaiting the blessed hope,

C'. ^{13b} the *appearance* of the glory of our great God and *savior* Jesus Christ,

B'. ¹⁴ who gave himself *on behalf of us*, so that he might redeem us from all lawlessness and cleanse for himself a special people, zealous for *commendable works*. ^{15a} These things *speak* and *exhort*

A'. ^{15b} and *reprove* with all command; let no one disregard you. ^{3:1} Remind them to submit to ruling authorities, to be obedient, to be ready *for all good work*, ² to blaspheme no one, to be unquarrelsome, kind, demonstrating all gentleness towards all *human beings*. ³ For we too were once ignorant, *disobedient*, misled, enslaved to various desires and pleasures, spending our lives in evil and envy, despicable, hating one another.[1]

CHIASTIC DEVELOPMENT FROM
TITUS 1:5–13A (B) TO 1:13B—3:3 (B')

With Titus 1:13b—3:3, the B' unit within the macrochiastic structure of Titus embracing the entire letter, the audience hear multiple echoes, by way of the chiastic parallelism, of 1:5–13a, the corresponding B unit in the overall chiasm. The command for the "younger women" to submit to "their own husbands (ἀνδράσιν)" in 2:5 of the B' unit recalls the stipulation for the elder to be the "husband (ἀνήρ) of one wife" in 1:6 of the B unit. That the opponent "may be put to shame, having (ἔχων) nothing bad to say about us" in 2:8 of the B' unit recalls that the elder must be "blameless . . . having (ἔχων) faithful children" in 1:6 of the B unit. The adjective "sensible" (σώφρονας) in 2:2 and 2:5, its verbal cognates (σωφρονίζωσιν, σωφρονεῖν) in 2:4 and 2:6, and its adverbial cognate (σωφρόνως) in 2:12 of the B' unit recall the quality of being "sensible" (σώφρονα) in 1:8 of the B unit. The repetition of the command to "exhort" (παρακάλει) in 2:6 and 2:15 of the B' unit recalls the elder's duty "to exhort" (παρακαλεῖν) in 1:9b of the B unit. Similarly, the repetition of the command to "reprove" (ἔλεγχε) in 1:13b and 2:15 of the B' unit recalls the elder's calling "to reprove" (ἐλέγχειν) in 1:9b of the B unit.

---

1. For the establishment of Titus 1:13b—3:3 as a chiasm, see ch. 2.

In addition to these parallels, the repeated references to "doctrine" (διδασκαλία) in 2:1, 2:7b, and 2:10b of the B' unit recall the reference to "doctrine" (διδασκαλία) in 1:9b of the B unit. Similarly, the various forms of "sound" (ὑγιαίνω) in 1:13b, 2:1, and 2:2 of the B' unit recall the participle "sound" (ὑγιαινούσῃ) in 1:9b of the B unit. Finally, that "slaves" are "to be pleasing, not those who oppose (ἀντιλέγοντας)" in 2:9 of the B' unit recalls "those who oppose" (ἀντιλέγοντας) in 1:9b of the B unit. The corresponding terms (above) occur uniquely in the B and B' units of the macrochiastic structure.

AUDIENCE RESPONSE TO TITUS 1:13B–3:3

1. Titus 1:13b-16 (A): Reprove the Defiled

This element begins with a stern command: "Therefore"—because "there are many rebels, empty-talkers and deceivers . . . who are upsetting whole households, teaching what is not necessary for this reason—shameful gain" (1:10–11)—Titus is to "reprove them severely" (1:13b).[2] The term "reprove" reminds the audience of the elder's basic calling to "reprove (ἐλέγχειν) those who oppose" (1:9b). That Titus is to do the work of the elder communicates to the audience that Titus is recognized already as "blameless" and is called to model the work of the elder. The adverb "severely" (ἀποτόμως) reiterates for the audience the gravity of the situation at hand, which, in turn, demands a response equal in weight. Indeed, the repetition of the verb "reprove" in such a short span of space illustrates for the audience what severe reproof is.

The purpose of the reproof is "so that (ἵνα) they might be sound (ὑγιαίνωσιν) in the faith." The conjunction "so that" (ἵνα) also echoes Paul's earlier statement in the B unit that the elder is to hold fast to the word, "so that (ἵνα) he might be able both to exhort with sound (ὑγιαινούσῃ) doctrine and reprove those who oppose." The message is

---

2. There is some uncertainty over the object (αὐτούς) of the reproof (see Knight, *Pastoral Epistles*, 299–300). On the surface the object seems obvious. Recalling the first occurrence of the verb, the audience identify the object as "those who oppose" (1:9b), the false teachers whom Paul specifies as "rebels, empty-talkers and deceivers" (1:10). The clause "upsetting whole households" and the present participle "teaching" (1:11), however, indicate that there are people among the audience who are currently submitting to and being misled by the opponents. It may be that the reproof is primarily for the false teachers, but applies secondarily to their followers; see Fee, *Titus*, 180; Marshall, *Pastoral Epistles*, 204–5.

clear: sound doctrine begets sound faith. Again, "faith" (πίστει) does not refer merely to the content of belief, but also to an embrace of the truth concerning eternal life that is accompanied by a godly lifestyle (1:1). Given the preceding context of the B unit, being "sound in the faith" means the opponents are to cease from teaching false doctrine for greedy gain.

Being sound in the faith entails "not paying attention to Jewish myths and commands of human beings who turn away from the truth" (1:14). Earlier the audience heard that the elder is "able both to exhort with sound doctrine and reprove those who oppose" by "holding fast (ἀντεχόμενον) to the faithful word that is according to the teaching" (1:9a). The verb "to hold fast to" carries the sense of extreme devotion and represents the "positive" means for being sound in the faith. In 1:14 the apostle presents the negative means for being "sound in the faith," namely by "not paying attention (προσέχοντες) to Jewish myths and regulations of human beings who turn away the truth." The verb "to pay attention to" also carries the sense of devotion, connoting the "giving of oneself."[3] Thus to "be sound in the faith" requires "paying attention" to "the faithful word that is according to the teaching" and "not paying attention" to anything that is antithetical to "sound doctrine."

Paul names two antitheses to sound teaching: "Jewish myths and regulations of human beings." While the apostle does not specify the content of "Jewish myths" ('Ιουδαϊκοῖς μύθοις), he has already established an association between the "rebels, empty-talkers and deceivers" and "the circumcision" (1:10). The "Jewish myths" in view, then, are the "myths" of those of "the circumcision." i.e., the false teaching of the opponents. Although Paul does not detail the content of the teaching, that he categorizes it as "myths"—"tales, stories, legends"[4]— indicates for the audience a clear contrast with the "truth" concerning the "hope of eternal life" (1:1b-2a). The second object is "regulations of human beings who turn away the truth." The "regulations" in view are human in nature and stand in contrast to the quality of Paul's "proclamation" (1:3). Paul can command with authority because he is a "slave of God and apostle of Jesus Christ" (1:1a) and because he ministers "according to the command of God" (1:3). In

3. Towner, *Letters*, 704: "It indicates obsession or belief, not simply a flirtation."

4. BDAG, s.v. While important Greek thinkers like Plato maintained that myths were sometimes helpful in teaching and promoting good behavior—much like any ancient fable—they did not believe that their actual content was always true; see, e.g., Plato *Resp.* 378.

contrast, these "regulations" stem from the authority of "human beings." What is most dangerous about these "regulations," however, is that they come from those "who turn away the truth." "Truth" (ἀλήθειαν) recalls for the audience Paul's calling from the "God, who cannot lie" (1:2b) to advance their "recognition of truth (ἀληθείας)" (1:1b) concerning the promise of eternal life. In contrast, these "human beings" are "turning away" from the truth and causing their followers to do the same. The only fitting response from the audience is to disregard both these human "regulations" and these apostate "human beings" if they wish to be "sound in the faith" (1:13).

In Titus 1:15a–16 the audience hear the verses as a mini-chiasm in itself. Verses 15a–16 are composed carefully of four sub-elements:

a. [15a] All things (πάντα) are clean to the clean

  b. [15b] But to the defiled (μεμιαμμένοις) and unfaithful nothing is clean;

  b'. [15c] rather, defiled (μεμίανται) are both their mind and conscience.

a'. [16] God they profess to know but by their works they deny, being vile and disobedient and unqualified for all (πᾶν) good work.

Through the parallel "a" and "a'" sub-elements the apostle sets up a strong contrast: on the one hand, "All things (πάντα) are clean to the clean" (1:15a); on the other hand, the hypocrites—those who "profess to know [God] but by their works they deny"—are "vile and disobedient and unqualified for all (πᾶν) good work" (1:16). The "b" and "b'" sub-elements share the common verb μιαίνω. Each sub-element of the mini-chiasm moves the audience closer to the climactic conclusion that the opponents are "vile."

Titus 1:15a (a)

The apostle is likely using a traditional saying in 1:15a–c to respond to the opponents' teaching concerning defilement. He begins by stating: "All things are clean to the clean." The adjective "clean" (καθαρός) refers to spiritual purity,[5] a condition arising not from one's own efforts but from divine election (1:1a) through which God forgives and redeems. For this reason, it is an apt description of the genuine believer's new existence.[6]

---

5. BDAG, s.v.

6. See Bassler, *Titus*, 190; Towner, *Goal of Our Instruction*, 159.

The totality of this inner renewal is indicated by the phrase "all things" (πάντα). Having experienced this divine and comprehensive cleansing, the audience recognize that nothing external— including the "regulations of human beings"—can make them unclean.

Titus 1:15b (b)

In the "b" sub-element of the mini-chiasm, the apostle declares that exactly the opposite is true for the opposing group, whom he categorizes as "defiled and unfaithful." The term "defiled" (μεμιαμμένοις) recalls for the audience its occurrences in the LXX where it denotes both ceremonial and moral defilement (e.g., Num 5:14; Ezek 4:14). In short, the condition represents the antithesis of being "clean." The opponents are further defined by the adjective "unfaithful" (ἀπίστοις). The adjective brings to the mind of the audience the several occurrences of "faith"—"the faith (πίστιν) of the elect" (1:1a), "the common faith (πίστιν)" (1:4), and "sound in the faith (πίστει)" (1:13)—which referred to the coupling of sound teaching and godly conduct. The alpha prefix in ἀπίστοις indicates to the audience that the "defiled" lack the genuine "faith" of the elect. For such a group, "nothing is clean" because no amount of observing human regulations can render them clean before God.[7]

Titus 1:15c (b')

Continuing his assessment of the "defiled and unfaithful," the apostle states: "rather, defiled are both their mind and conscience." At this point the audience hear the pivot of this mini-chiasm from a general indictment of being "defiled" (μεμιαμμένοις) in the "b" sub-element to the specification that "both their mind and conscience" are "defiled" (μεμίανται) in the "b'" sub-element. The conjunction "rather" (ἀλλά) and the priority of the adjective in the sentence accentuate further for the audience that "nothing is clean" for the "unfaithful." Within Paul's anthropology, the "mind" (νοῦς) perceives truth while the "conscience" (συνείδησις) refers to the inward faculty of discerning between good and evil;[8] the latter analyzes the data provided by the former.[9] That "both their mind and

---

7. See Towner, *Letters*, 708.

8. BDAG, s.v.

9. See Harris, "Syneidesis (conscience) in the Pauline Writings," 173–86; Jewett, *Paul's Anthropological Terms*, 412–26; Stelzenberger, *Syneidesis im Neuen Testament*, 51–95; Stepień, "Syneidesis," 1–20.

conscience are "defiled (μεμίανται)" focuses the audience away from the opponents' general depravity to their specific deficiency concerning truth; in a word, they lack the basic faculties to recognize truth. As such, they are appropriately referred to as "human beings who turn away from the truth" (1:14).

Titus 1:16 (a')

The apostle concludes the mini-chiasm with a final and devastating assessment of the opponents: "God they profess to know but by their works they deny." The statement exhibits a particular rhythm, following the sequence of an object followed by a verb ending in ai: θεὸν ὁμολογοῦσιν εἰδέναι, τοῖς δὲ ἔργοις ἀρνοῦνται. This rhythmic pattern allows for the indictment to be all the more jarring and memorable to the audience.

The verb "profess" (ὁμολογοῦσιν) connotes a public and solemn claim.[10] The verb echoes the earlier occurrences of "word"—"his word (λόγον)" (1:3) and the "faithful word (λόγου) that is according to the teaching"—and creates a noticeable irony for the audience. While the word of God is reliable, the solemn claim of the opponents proves unreliable. The irony is amplified, given that the "God" (θεόν) they profess" is the "God (θεός), who cannot lie" (1:2). The irony is amplified further through the verb "to know" (εἰδέναι), which indicates an intimate relationship.[11] It is clear that the opponents do not have the privileged status of Paul, who is a "slave of God and apostle of Jesus Christ" (1:1) despite their high claims. Such an empty profession of faith advances the audience's understanding of Paul's earlier condemnation of the opponents as "empty-talkers" (ματαιολόγοι).

The second half of the charge, "but by their works they deny," makes explicit what was implied by the earlier description of how the opponents are teaching what they should not for shameful gain (1:11); in short, their "works" (ἔργοις) invalidate their profession of faith.[12] This was also implied in the apostle's earlier statement that the "recognition of the truth" must be accompanied by "godliness" (1:1a). The audience now hear the corollary to that statement—that the absence of works negates any claim to know God.

10. See Fee, *Titus*, 182; Quinn, *Letter*, 114; Spicq, *Les Épîtres Pastorales*, 613.

11. BDAG, s.v.

12. Marshall, *Pastoral Epistles*, 212: "ἔργον . . . is used in the PE especially to refer to the outward deeds which demonstrate faith or the lack of it."

Verse 16 concludes with a devastating condemnation: they are "vile and disobedient and unqualified for every good work." The first adjective "vile" (βδελυκτοί) denotes someone/something repugnant or detestable and is an appropriate description of these hypocrites. The second adjective "disobedient" (ἀπειθεῖς) advances the earlier descriptor "rebels" (ἀνυπότακτοι, 1:10). "Rebels" highlights their insubordinate attitude; "disobedient" highlights their defiant actions.

Finally, the phrase "unqualified for all good work" contrasts for the audience the opponents, who are "unqualified" (ἀδόκιμοι), with the elder, who has proven he is "above reproach" (ἀνέγκλητος, 1:6, 7), i.e., who is qualified in every sense. In addition, while the elder is a "lover-of-good" (φιλάγαθον), the opponents are "unqualified for all good (ἀγαθόν) work."[13] The adjective "all" (πᾶν) not only expresses the totality of their disqualification, but it also reminds the audience of the apostle's earlier statement, "All things (πάντα) are clean to the clean." Through the chiastic parallelism, the audience perceive that being qualified for "all good work" is characteristic of believers, not hypocrites.

2. Titus 2:1–10a (B): Exhort the Household of God [14]

In Titus 2:1–10a the audience hear the B element of the third chiastic unit (1:13b—3:3) as a mini-chiasm in itself. Verses 1–10a are composed carefully of five sub-elements:

13. Witherington (*Letters*, 127) provides a helpful summary comparison between the elder and false teachers:

Elder	False Teacher
house manager	house wrecker
blameless	defiled conscience and works
not pursuing dishonest gain	unscrupulous teaching for gain
not quick-tempered or intemperate	acting like a wild beast
holding fast to sound tradition	embracing myths and human commands
truthful and refuting error	liar, deceiver, embracing and teaching error

14. Witherington (ibid., 130–32) cautions against concluding that 2:1–10a represents a "modified household code"; cf. Johnson, *Letters*, 232–33. While recognizing these nuances, Titus 1:7 indicates that the Church is to be viewed by the audience as the household of God; see Matera, *New Testament Theology*, 249–52.

a. $^{2:1}$ But you speak what is consistent with sound doctrine (ὑγιαινούσῃ διδασκαλίᾳ).

^{2} Older men are to be temperate, serious (σεμνούς), sensible, sound (ὑγιαίνοντας) in faith (πίστει), in love, and in endurance.

b. ^{3} Older women, similarly (ὡσαύτως), are to be reverent in behavior, not slanderers, not enslaved to much wine, commendable teachers, ^{4} so that they may make sensible the younger women (νέας) to be lovers-of-husbands, lovers-of-children, ^{5a} sensible, chaste, homemakers, good, submitting to their own husbands,

c. ^{5b} so that the word of God may not be blasphemed.

b'. ^{6} Exhort the younger men (νεωτέρους) to be similarly (ὡσαύτως) sensible

^{7a} about all things,

a'. ^{7b} presenting yourself as a model of commendable works, in the doctrine (διδασκαλίᾳ) incorruption, seriousness (σεμνότητα), ^{8} sound (ὑγιῆ) word that is beyond reproach, so that the opponent may be put to shame, having nothing bad to say about us. ^{9} Slaves are to submit to their own masters in all things, to be pleasing, not those who oppose, ^{10a} not those who pilfer; rather those who demonstrate that all faith (πίστιν) is good,

The B element contains the apostle's exhortations which Titus is to "speak" to the various members of God's household "so that the word of God may not be blasphemed" (2:5b). By receiving and applying these exhortations, the audience live differently from Cretan society and from the hypocritical opponents (1:16). Titus is to carry out these exhortations by speaking "what is consistent with sound doctrine" (2:1), exhorting with sound doctrine (2:6) and presenting himself as a "model of commendable works" (2:7b). The multiple linguistic parallels between the corresponding sub-elements highlight the unity of this mini-chiasm. According to the conclusion of the mini-chiasm Titus's exhortations and the positive response of the audience will "demonstrate that all faith is good."

Titus 2:1–2 (a)

The "a" sub-element begins with the words "But you" (σὺ δέ). With these words Paul contrasts Titus and—indirectly—the Cretan community with those who need to be reproved severely in 1:13b of the A element.

Succinctly but powerfully Paul says, "But you" are to be different from those who are not "sound in the faith" (1:13b), "who turn away the truth" (1:14), who are "defiled and unfaithful" (1:15), and who "profess to know [God] but by their works they deny."[15]

The phrase "sound doctrine" (ὑγιαινούσῃ διδασκαλίᾳ) recollects for the audience the elder's task to "exhort with sound doctrine (τῇ διδασκαλίᾳ τῇ ὑγιαινούσῃ)." The audience infer, therefore, that the verb "speak" (λάλει) is synonymous with "exhort" and that Titus is commanded to carry out presently the work expected of future elders. The object of the verb "speak" is "what is consistent (ἃ πρέπει) with sound doctrine," and it amplifies for the audience the apostle's concern for commendable works. Holding fast to sound doctrine is, of course, required of the elder (1:9a), but the ultimate purpose is that by doing so he may exhort and reprove believers to good works (1:9b). Similarly, here the apostle's concern for godliness is reiterated for the audience by the carefully crafted exhortation. Instead of saying, "Speak sound doctrine," he commands, "Speak what is consistent with sound doctrine," i.e., delineate the kind of lifestyle that is fitting with sound doctrine. Indeed, the repetition of "sound" in such a short span of space (1:9b, 13b; 2:1) emphasizes for the audience the importance of teaching what is beneficial and healthy instead of "teaching what is not necessary" (1:11), as is the practice of the opponents.

There are five groups whom Titus is to speak to, divided according to gender, age, and socio-economic class. First, Titus is to address the "older men" (πρεσβύτας): "Older men are to be temperate, serious, sensible, sound in faith, in love, in endurance."[16] In the qualities for the "blameless" elder he underscored the elder's ability to lead his own household well (1:6). The parallelism between the elder and "older men" is indicated by the repetition of the quality "sensible" in 1:8 and 2:2.[17] The "older men," as

---

15. It is common to treat 1:10–16 as a single unit. The inclusion of 1:13b–16 into the third microchiasm, however, is not only linguistically defensible (see ch. 2) but also rhetorically significant. Comprising of 1:13b–16, the A element of the third microchiasm provides a vivid contrast against which Titus and the audience are to understand themselves and the exhortations that follow in 2:1–10a. Comprising of 1:10–13a, the A' element of the second microchiasm (1:5–13a) provides a vivid contrast for the blameless elder in view in 1:5–8, the A element.

16. The minimal age required to be in this group is difficult to determine. Towner (*Letters*, 720) suggests above forty.

17. Nevertheless, Paul is careful to use the different term πρεσβύτας in 2:2 from

"fathers" of God's household, are to be the spiritual leaders and thus are the first to receive exhortations.

The first adjective "temperate" (νηφαλίους) refers to moderation in alcohol consumption[18] and reminds the audience both of the elder who should not be a "drunkard" (πάροινον, 1:7) and the false teachers who are "gluttons" (γαστέρες, 1:12). That alcoholism was a prevalent problem in the Greco-Roman world, especially among the elderly, makes this quality especially pointed for the audience.[19] The second adjective "serious" (σεμνούς) expresses, both in Jewish and Greco-Roman literature, respectable public conduct and speech (e.g., Prov 8:6; Herodotus *Hist.* 2.173). The third adjective "sensible" (σώφρονας) conveys a sense of balance and thoughtfulness, and echoes the third positive quality of the elder who is to be sensible (σώφρονα, 1:8). The repetition of the adjective communicates to the audience that blameless behavior is expected of all who belong to the "elect of God" (1:1a), not just of the elder.

The fourth quality is "sound in faith, in love, and in endurance." The triad of faith, love, and endurance not only provides the audience with a sense of balance with the three preceding adjectives "temperate, serious, sensible," but also communicates to the audience the comprehensive quality of being sound. The phrase "sound in faith" (ὑγιαίνοντας τῆ πίστει), in particular, recalls for the audience the opponents who need to be reproved in order to be "sound in the faith" (ὑγιαίνωσιν ἐν τῆ πίστει). As noted in the preceding chapters, to be "sound in faith" includes both holding fasting to sound doctrine and living according to godliness. "Love" (ἀγάπη) accompanies "faith" in God because it expresses visibly the invisible—sacrificial good works in the present on account of eternal glory.[20] Through love, the "older men" demonstrate the sincerity of their "faith," distinguishing themselves from the apostates of 1:16. "Endurance" (ὑπομονῆ) completes the triad and reminds the audience again of the elder who is to hold fast to the faithful word even when others do not. In the immediate context, the presence and influence of false teachers and apostates indicate a setting charged with

---

πρεσβυτέρους in 1:5 to highlight that a church office is in view earlier in the letter; see Quinn, *Letter*, 117.

18. BDAG, s.v.

19. See Witherington, *Letters*, 134–35, esp. his references to multiple ancient sources.

20. See Schrage, *The Ethics of the New Testament*, 211–17.

conflict. To maintain "faith" and "love" will require tremendous fortitude and steadfastness.

Titus 2:3–5a (b)

The next sub-element in this mini-chiasm focuses on the women in the audience. First, the apostle addresses the "older women" (πρεσβύτιδας): "Older women, similarly, are to be reverent in behavior." Like the "older men" they are to express their "faith" in action by being "reverent in behavior." The adverb "similarly" (ὡσαύτως) indicates to the audience that the same standard of godliness is expected of both genders despite their distinct roles. The adjective "reverent" (ἱεροπρεπεῖς) combines the words ἱερός and πρέπω. In the LXX, ἱερός connotes holiness either with respect to God or the temple.[21] The term πρέπω reminds the audience of Paul's command to "speak what is consistent (πρέπει) with sound doctrine" (2:1). The adjective ἱεροπρεπεῖς, then, expresses the quality of being consistent with holiness. This quality is to be expressed concretely "in behavior" (ἐν καταστήματι). Again, the audience sense a clear call to live differently from the opponents whose behavior invalidates their faith (1:16).

Reverence in behavior is to be expressed in three ways. The first two are expressed negatively: "not slanders, not enslaved to much wine." It is likely that Paul is addressing the "stereotypical and current critical profile of older wives who were prone to drunkenness and loose talk."[22] The term "slanderers" (διαβόλους) focuses on the speech of the older women. It is also the main title in the NT for the "devil" (διάβολος), the "entity opposed to the divine will,"[23] who oftentimes expresses his opposition through slanderous speech. In this sense, it is a fitting description of the false teachers and apostates described in 1:10–13a and 1:13b–16, and the command not to be "slanderers" is another exhortation not to be like the opposition. The expression "not enslaved to much wine (οἴνῳ)" echoes the requirement for an "elder" not to be a "drunkard" (πάροινον) and the requirement for "older men" to be "temperate," i.e., moderate in their consummation of alcohol. Again, by extending this virtue to the "older women," the apostle is underscoring for the audience that rather than

---

21. See BDAG, s.v.

22. Towner, *Letters*, 723 nn. 33–39. See also Dover, *Greek Popular Morality*, 95–102.

23. BDAG, s.v.

being "enslaved (δεδουλωμένας) to much wine," like Paul, who is a "slave (δοῦλος) of God," they are to live under the rule of a different master.

The more common translation for καλοδιδασκάλους is "teaching what is good (e.g., *NAB*, *ESV*), and it highlights "what" is taught versus "who" teaches. The preceding expressions in 2:3, however, focus more on character than action; thus, the translation "commendable teachers" is to be preferred. The prefix καλός denotes "what is attractive in outward appearance"[24] and communicates the kind of "teacher" (διδάσκαλος) that "older women" should aspire to be. By displaying reverence, sound speech, and temperance, they present themselves as "teachers" who are "attractive in outward appearance." In this way, the audience understand that the "older women" are to distinguish themselves from the "rebels, empty-talkers and deceivers" (1:10) who are "teaching (διδάσκοντες) what is not necessary for this reason—shameful gain" (1:11) and, instead, identify themselves with the elder who is blameless (1:6–8) and holds fast to the "faithful word that is according to the teaching (διδαχήν)" (1:9a) so that he might be able both to exhort with sound doctrine (διδασκαλία) and reprove those who oppose" (1:9b).

In 2:4–5, Paul begins his discussion on the "younger women" (νέας) by relating it to the previous exhortation to the "older women" to reverent "commendable teachers": "so that they might make sensible (σωφρονίζωσιν) the younger women." The verb σωφρονίζωσιν echoes its adjectival cognate "sensible" in 1:8 (σώφρονα) concerning the elder and in 2:2 (σώφρονας) concerning the "older men." Here it seems to carry the nuance of reproof—"the idea of a figurative, sobering 'slap in the face' (i.e., 'to bring someone back to his/her senses')."[25] The verb suggests that the "younger women" are no longer "sensible," presumably as a result of the false teaching described in 1:10–13a. They have become like faithless "children . . . in accusation of debauchery or rebellious" (1:6). The older women, therefore, must reprove them so that they may be sound once again in the faith.

The first two qualities that the apostle enumerates are "lovers-of-husbands" (φιλάνδρους) and "lovers-of-children" (φιλοτέκνους). The common prefix suggests that these two qualities should be taken to-

---

24. BDAG, s.v.

25. Towner, *Letters*, 725. For examples of this use of the verb in ancient Jewish literature, see Winter, *Roman Wives*, 154–59. Winter highlights how these sources use this verb versus other more neutral didactic terms to express the sense of reproof.

gether, conveying that the "younger women" should be "lovers-of-family." The audience intuit a deliberate connection between the elder and the "younger women." In describing the "blameless" elder, the apostle focused on his relationship to his spouse and children (1:6). In a similar fashion the apostle accents here the relationship to the spouse and children. In addition, the qualities φιλάνδρους and φιλοτέκνους are followed by the adjective σώφρονας (2:5). This sequence echoes the earlier sequence φιλόξενον, φιλάγαθον, σώφρονα (1:8) regarding the elder. Thus the audience understand that even the "younger women" are to be like the "blameless" elders. In this way the audience are reminded again that all are expected to act in accordance to godliness even though this is expected especially of the elders.

In 2:5a Paul lists the remaining five qualities that "younger women" must cultivate: they must be "sensible, chaste, homemakers, good, submitting to their own husbands."[26] The references to "sensible" (σώφρονας) and "husbands" (ἀνδράσιν) reiterate the verb "make sensible" (σωφρονίζωσιν) and adjective "lovers-of-husbands" (φιλάνδρους) in 2:4. Like the elder and "older men" who must be "sensible" (σώφρονα, 1:8; σώφρονας, 2:2) the "younger women" must exhibit self-restraint and prudence; but the apostle's use of "sensible" in this instance applies specifically to the household: the "younger women" are to be "sensible" as they reflect on and fulfill their duties as wives and mothers.[27] Similarly,

26. The precise number of qualities in view is not entirely clear. For example, Fee (*Titus*, 187), Knight (*Pastoral Epistles*, 308), and Marshall (*Pastoral Epistles*, 246) group the first six items in pairs given the lexical similarities between the first two terms (φιλάνδρους/φιλοτέκνους). Such pairing seems unwarranted because the latter two pairs do not share such similarities. Moreover, such lexical similarities are found in 1:8 (φιλόξενον/φιλάγαθον), but in that instance there was no reason for pairing the other qualities that follow. Moreover, it is not uncommon to translate οἰκουργοὺς ἀγαθάς as a single quality ("good homemakers," *NAB*). The syntax, however, favors viewing ἀγαθάς as a distinct virtue; see Marshall, *Pastoral Epistles*, 249. Hence, "working at home, kind" (*ESV*), "fulfilling their duties at home, kind" (*NET*). The profile of the "younger women," then, consists of seven descriptors.

While the precise age of this group is also difficult to determine, the context makes clear that the apostle has in view women who are still young enough to have children and whose basic domestic duty at this stage of their lives is to be good homemakers by caring for their husbands and children in contrast to the "older women" whose husbands may no longer be alive and whose children are able to care for themselves.

27. Winter (*Romans Wives*, 101–2) argues that the adjective pertained directly to public conduct and dress that would display modesty and honor the husband's reputation.

while the adjective "chaste" (ἀγνάς) can refer to general righteousness (e.g., Prov 20:9), here, it likely connotes marital fidelity.

The adjective "homemakers" (οἰκουργούς) combines the two terms "home" (οἶκος) and "work" (ἔργον) and connotes the diligent carrying out of household duties.[28] Again, the connection with the elder is reinforced, who is described as a "household-manager" (οἰκονόμον; 1:7). The adjective "good" (ἀγαθάς)—standing alone—expresses kindness: "the wife is to exhibit kindness towards all those with whom she comes in contact as she applies herself to her domestic duties."[29] Finally, the apostle states that "younger women" should be "submitting to their own husbands." The participle "submitting" (ὑποτασσομένας) involves the recognition of an ordered structure.[30] The apostle desires for the "younger women" to be like "faithful children not in accusation of debauchery or rebellious" (1:6)—who recognize the ordered structure of the family, and unlike "rebels" (1:10) who disregard the ordered structure of the household of God. The adjective "own" (ἰδίοις) limits the stipulation to the relationship between husband and wife. All in all the audience perceive that, according to the apostle, becoming sensible for the younger women entails being sensible about order in the domestic household and cognizant of their unique roles.

Titus 2:5b (c)

According to the pivot of this mini-chiasm (2:5b) the purpose (ἵνα) for reproving the "younger women" is "so that the word God may not be blasphemed." That the "word of God may not be blasphemed" is pregnant with meaning, progressing the audience's understanding both of the "word" and Paul's antipathy for the false teachers and apostates. The verb "blasphemed" (βλασφημῆται) means to speak in an insulting, demeaning, and irreverent manner. The term occurs regularly in the LXX to describe the words of Gentiles who mocked God on account of Israel's failings. The term expresses more than a failure to acknowledge and revere God as God; it includes ridicule and scorn for the name and reliability of Israel's God.

28. BDAG, s.v.

29. Marshall, *Pastoral Epistles*, 249.

30. BDAG, s.v.

The focus in 2:5b, however, is on the "word of God" (ὁ λόγος τοῦ θεοῦ). The audience know from the first microchiasm (1:1–4) that the "word of God" is the "word" that has been "revealed" in the apostle's "proclamation" from the "God, who cannot lie" concerning the "hope of eternal life." The emphasis in the first microchiasm is twofold—the source of the "word" is transcendent but the means are historical and concrete, manifested in Paul's ministry. The audience also know that this "word" is the "faithful word" (πιστοῦ λόγου, 1:9a), i.e., the believable words that Christians believe in. Yet, despite its inherent reliable nature and its faithful transmission through Paul, the audience perceive now that the "word of God" can be ridiculed and ultimately rejected on account of any believer's conduct, not just that of the elder. That this is the case deepens the audience's appreciation for the apostle's concern and emphasis on living commendably. In short, the audience recognize the profound ramifications of their actions on the reception of the "word of God."

Titus 2:6–7a (b')

The command concerning the "younger men" is concise but no less comprehensive than the previous exhortations, for they are told "to be sensible about all things." The adverb "similarly" (ὡσαύτως) communicates to the audience that the "younger men" (νεωτέρους) are—like the "younger women" (νέας)—to be "sensible" (σωφρονεῖν) about being lovers-of-wives, lovers-of-children, and other domestic duties unique to their gender. In addition, the adverb recalls for the audience its earlier occurrence in 2:3 where Paul commands, "Older women, similarly (ὡσαύτως), are to be reverent in behavior." In that instance, "older women" were coupled with "older men." Thus, the audience sense a clear correspondence between the "older men" and "the older women," and between the "younger men" and the "younger women." Moreover, the repetition of the adverb highlights that sensibility is a virtue that is expected of all believers, regardless of age or gender. That the "younger men" are to be sensible about "all things" (πάντα) communicates to the audience that the "younger men" have a more extended array of responsibilities than the "younger women" although the exhortation concerning them is shorter.

Titus 2:7b–10a (a')

The final sub-element contains exhortations for Titus and "slaves." The command to "exhort the younger men . . ." is coupled with the participial phrase "showing yourself as a model of commendable works." The participle παρεχόμενος means to "show oneself" in a way that "causes other people to experience something."³¹ The term τύπον signifies a "model" that is to be imitated. Titus is to be a "model" of "commendable works" (καλῶν ἔργων) for the "younger men," i.e., "works" that are not only useful but also readily observable as attractive and admirable. The audience experience a chiastic progression at this juncture. Titus is to be like the "older women" who are "commendable teachers" (καλοδιδασκάλους), patterning for the "younger women" reverent behavior, holy speech, and self-control (2:3). Like the "younger women" who follow the "model of commendable works" of "older women," the "younger men" are to follow the example of Titus, their "commendable teacher. In addition, Titus is to embody the antithesis of the apostates who are "unqualified for all good work (ἔργον)" (1:16). Unlike this group that professes to know God but deny him by their "works" (ἔργοις), Titus is to demonstrate that his "recognition of truth" accords with "godliness" (1:1a).

In 2:7b-8a the apostle focuses on the model that Titus is to set with respect to doctrine: "in the doctrine incorruption, seriousness." "Doctrine" (διδασκαλία) recalls for the audience the parallel activities of exhorting and speaking—the elder must "exhort with sound doctrine (διδασκαλία)" (1:9b) and Titus must "speak what is consistent with sound doctrine (διδασκαλία)" (2:1). Concerning this sound doctrine, Titus must exemplify the qualities of "incorruption" and "seriousness." The concrete meaning of both terms is indicated in the preceding sections. "Incorruption" (ἀφθορίαν) is often translated as "integrity" (e.g., NAB, ESV, NET). Its cognate adjective ἄφθορος is used to describe an innocent and pure individual. It reminds the audience of Paul's indictment in 1:15 which contains the assonances to ἀφθορίαν in the term "pure": "All things are clean (καθαρά) to the clean (καθαροῖς). But to the defiled and unfaithful nothing is clean (καθαρόν)." In contrast to the "rebels, empty-talkers and deceivers" (1:10) who teach for "shameful gain," Titus is to have pure motives when promulgating doctrine. In addition, like the "older men" who should be "serious" (σεμνούς, 2:2), Titus is to conduct himself in a respectable manner that accords with sound doctrine.

In addition to these qualities, Titus's "doctrine" must be characterized by "sound word that is beyond reproach." The "sound word"

31. BDAG, s.v.

(λόγον ὑγιῆ) is the "word (λόγος) of God" (2:5) concerning the "hope of eternal life" revealed in Paul's proclamation" (1:2a–3). It is the "faithful word (λόγου)" (1:9a) to which the elder must "hold fast." Like "sound (ὑγιαινούσῃ) doctrine" (1:9b; 2:1) the "sound (ὑγιῆ) word" is that which imparts health to the audience. The adjective "beyond reproach" (ἀκατάγνωστον) is found in legal contexts and has the sense of "abiding by the terms of a contract."[32] The audience understand the adjective as a reference to "abiding by the terms" of the word that has been entrusted to Paul (1:3), which is the "word of God."

In 2:8b the apostle states the purpose (ἵνα) for Titus's model: "so that the opponent (ὁ ἐξ ἐναντίας) may be put to shame." The audience heard the apostle describe "rebels, empty-talkers and deceivers" as "the circumcision (οἱ ἐκ)" (1:10). Also, the audience heard the apostle describe the Cretan prophet as "one of (τις ἐξ) them" (1:13a). Thus, they know that the apostle distinguishes between groups and individuals when necessary. Here, then, the audience hear the phrase "the opponent" (ὁ ἐξ ἐναντίας) as a reference to a specific individual, although an entire group is in view by association.[33] The phrase evx evnanti,aj occurs regularly in the LXX to express a location that is "on the opposite side" or an attack "against" an enemy (e.g., Exod 14:2; Josh 8:11; 1 Sam 17:2). This individual, then, is one who stands "opposite" of or "against" Paul and is among the false teachers and hypocritical apostates (1:10–16).

Titus's commitment to character and content will result in the opponent's being "put to shame, having nothing bad to say about us." The sense of the verb "put to shame" (ἐντραπῇ) is to be stripped of all confidence. The implication is that the opponent will have "nothing bad to say about us" because of the believers' godly conduct. The audience perceive that the participle ἔχων bears an authoritative quality. The elder's "having (ἔχων) faithful children" (1:6) according to the B microchiastic unit testifies to his leadership abilities. The participle in 2:8 occurs with the noun "nothing" (μηδέν) and thus communicates to the audience that the opponent has nothing legitimate to "say about us." The apostle also reiterates Titus's representative role through the phase "about us" (περὶ ἡμῶν). For this reason, both his words and deeds (2:7b-8) must strip the opponent

---

32. Towner, *Letters*, 733 n. 80.
33. Ibid., 734; see also Witherington, *Letters*, 140 n. 166.

of any basis for speaking badly about Paul, Titus, and the "elect." In short, Titus is to be "blameless."

Bringing this mini-chiasm to a close, Paul addresses the "slaves" (δούλους). They "are to submit to their own masters in all things" unlike the "rebels" (ἀνυπότακτοι, 1:10) who show contempt for authority. Masters are those who have "legal control and authority" over the "slaves."[34] "Slaves," then, "are to submit to their own masters" (ἰδίοις δεσπόταις ὑποτάσσεσθαι) for the same reason Paul, as a "slave (δοῦλος) of God" (1:1a) submits to the command of his savior (1:3) and for the same reason "younger women" are to be "submitting (ὑποτασσομένας) to their own (ἰδίοις) husbands" (2:5a)—out of recognition of legitimate authority. The exhortation to be submissive "in all things" (ἐν πᾶσιν) echoes the command for the "younger men . . . to be similarly sensible about all things (πάντα)" (2:6–7a).

The nature of their submission is specified in the complementary phrases that follow: "to be pleasing, not those who oppose" and "not those who pilfer; rather those who demonstrate that all faith is good." The use of such complements reiterates the author's style to state the negative (e.g., what an elder should not be; 1:7) and the positive (e.g., what an elder should be; 1:8), so that the audience have a comprehensive understanding of the subject at hand.

In the Greco-Roman world, the adjective "pleasing" (εὐαρέστους) referred to individuals known for their "civic-minded generosity"[35] and who were consequently esteemed by the general public. Slaves are to submit to their masters in a manner that renders their service not only acceptable but also respectable. In addition, slaves are not to be "those who oppose" (ἀντιλέγοντας). The participle recalls for the audience the elder's calling to "exhort with sound doctrine and reprove those who oppose (ἀντιλέγοντας)" (1:9b). This group's rebellion is described initially with a focus on their words ("empty-talkers . . . whom it is necessary to silence," 1:10–11). "To be pleasing, not those who oppose" thus communicates to the slaves the prohibition against "talking back to them" (NAB, NET) and being "argumentative" (ESV). Similarly, Paul's complementary style here communicates to the audience that "those who oppose" in 1:9b

---

34. BDAG, s.v.

35. BDAG, s.v.

are conducting themselves in a less than respectable manner, thus bring disrepute to the word of God.

The second pair of complementary phrases exhorts the "slaves" not to be "those who pilfer." The participle νοσφίζομαι covers a wide range of thievery, including stealing the possession of others or misappropriating resources from their intended use.[36] It was generally known that slaves would pilfer to improve gradually their situation.[37] Instead of falling prey to this common temptation, Christian "slaves" are to be people "who demonstrate that all faith is good."[38] The meaning of "all faith" is clear simply from the apostle's use of "faith." According to 1:1a, Paul is an "apostle of Jesus Christ according to the faith (πίστιν) of the elect of God," i.e., "their recognition of truth according to godliness" (1:1b). "Faith," then, is all-encompassing, impacting the mind and behavior. Similarly, the "false teachers, empty-talkers and deceivers" (1:10) are unsound "in the faith (πίστει)" (1:13b) not only because they are "teaching what is not necessary" but also because they are teaching for "shameful gain" (1:11). Their "faith" is fallen on both grounds. Similarly, the "older men" are exhorted to be sound in the faith (πίστει)" (2:2), a faith established from instruction in "sound doctrine" (2:1) and exhibited in action (2:2). "All faith," therefore, refers to "faith" that is complete—"faith" that is genuine because it demonstrates a "recognition of truth according to godliness."[39] Against the suspicion that the Christian faith will be a disruptive force for society, "slaves" are to demonstrate that authentic "faith"

36. See Kelly, *Pastoral Epistles*, 243.

37. See Quinn, *Letter*, 149.

38. The translation of the phrase πᾶσαν πίστιν ἐνδεικνυμένους ἀγαθήν is difficult because the force of ἀγαθήν is unclear. Is it attributive (see *NAB, ESV, NET*) or predicate (see above)? Either interpretation can fit with the text, but the uncommon translation above follows the Greek more carefully. Daniel B. Wallace (*The Basics of New Testament Syntax*, 86, 139) understands this phrase as an example of a verb that takes an object-complement combination.

39. Most commentators maintain that pi,stin in 2:10a refers to the virtue of being "trustworthy" (see, e.g., Fee, *Titus*, 191; Marshall, *Pastoral Epistles*, 260; Quinn, *Letter*, 149; Towner, *Letters*, 737). Undoubtedly a contrast with the unreliable character of "those who pilfer" is in view. But something akin to the anacoluthon of 1:2–3 seems to be occurring here, because the object of the verb ἐνδεικνυμένους is "all faith" versus the slaves themselves. Implicitly the "slaves" must prove "reliable," but the apostle's focus here is on the "faith" that produces trustworthy individuals. To miss this nuance by focusing on the character rather than the faith that produces it is to miss Paul's specific and main concern for authentic faith in the letter to Titus.

is "good"; that those with "all faith"—the "clean"—are qualified "for all good (ἀγαθόν) work" and can, therefore, be counted completely trustworthy by their masters.[40]

3. Titus 2:10b-12 (C): The Doctrine of the Grace of God

In Titus 2:10b-12 the audience hear the C element of the third chiastic unit (1:13b–3:3) as a mini-chiasm in itself. Verses 10b-12 are composed carefully of three sub-elements:

> a. [10b] so that they might adorn (κοσμῶσιν) the doctrine of God our savior (σωτῆρος) in all things (πᾶσιν).
>
> b. [11a] For the grace of God has appeared,
>
> a'. [11b] saving (σωτήριος) all (πᾶσιν) human beings [12] training us, so that by denying ungodliness and worldly (κοσμικὰς) desires we might live sensibly and righteously and godly in the present age,

This mini-chiasm centers on the saving grace of the saving God, which, in turn, dictates how the believers are to live "in the present age." In view of "the grace of God [that] has appeared," Titus and the Cretan community are to "live sensibly and righteously and godly in the present age." The "a" and "a'" sub-elements share three linguistic parallels—"adorn" (κοσμῶσιν) and "worldly" (κοσμικὰς), "savior" (σωτῆρος) and "saving" (σωτήριος), and "all things" (πᾶσιν) and "all (πᾶσιν) human beings." The pivot of the mini-chiasm declares, "For the grace of God has appeared."

Titus 2:10b (a)

In the C element of the third microchiasm the apostle articulates the soteriological basis for Christian conduct. He first states the purpose (ἵνα) for godliness among slaves: "so that they might adorn the doctrine of God our savior in all things." The direct correlation between the conduct of "slaves" and the reputation of the "doctrine of God our savior" is evidenced in the exact repetition of the phrase "in all things" (ἐν πᾶσιν): their submission "in all things" (2:9) will "adorn the doctrine of God our savior in all things (ἐν πᾶσιν)." By being submissive "in all things," positively the "doctrine of God our savior" is adorned "in all things," negatively the opponent has

---

40. Again many commentators offer a different interpretation for ἀγαθήν, suggesting that it limits the scope of the slaves submission to only what is good; see Marshall, *Pastoral Epistles*, 261; Quinn, *Letter*, 149. This line of interpretation misses the point of the entire expression.

"nothing bad to say about us" (1:8). Thus, even "slaves" play a vital role in preserving and propagating the reputation of believers and their faith.

The verb "adorn" (κοσμῶσιν) means to "make beautiful and attractive."[41] Like the "younger women" who must submit to their "own husbands, so that the word of God may not be blasphemed" (2:5a), and like Titus who must present himself as a "model of commendable works . . . so that the opponent might be put to shame, having nothing bad to say about us" (2:6–8), "slaves" must "submit to their own masters in all things . . . so that they may adorn the doctrine of God our savior in all things." The first two purpose clauses (ἵνα), which were stated negatively, prepare the audience for this climactic and positive purpose clause. They are reminded that just as the elder's life must be characterized by the absence of negative qualities and the presence of positive qualities (1:7–8), so too their conduct must—negatively—guard the "word of God" from blasphemy and—positively—"adorn the doctrine of God our savior."

The object of the verb "adorn" is "doctrine" (διδασκαλίαν), the very "doctrine" (διδασκαλίᾳ) that provides the basis for the teaching, exhorting, and reproving activities of the elder (1:9b) and Titus, the model elder (2:1, 7). Paul specifies "doctrine" as the "doctrine of God our savior (τοῦ σωτῆρος ἡμῶν θεοῦ)." This description recalls for the audience God's "word in proclamation," with which Paul was "considered faithful according to the command of God our savior (τοῦ σωτῆρος ἡμῶν θεοῦ)" (1:3). The audience are thus reminded of the importance of the theme of salvation in this letter. In addition, the audience clearly understand now that "doctrine" is not just about "God our savior" written by human beings, but it is also from "God our savior," just as the "word" is the "word of God" (1:3; 2:5). For this reason, it is naturally "sound" (1:9b; 2:7), i.e., that which benefits the audience and should be accompanied by "incorruption, seriousness" (2:7).

Titus 2:11a (b)

In 2:11a the apostle begins to provide the basis for the conduct that was outlined in 2:1–10a: "For the grace of God has appeared." In 1:4 the term "grace" (χάρις) expresses divine empowerment to pursue "godliness"; hence, the apostle wished "grace" for the audience. Here, Paul progresses the audience's understanding of "grace" by reminding them of the "grace

---

41. BDAG, s.v.

of God" that "has appeared." The verb ἐπιφάνη generally indicates the tangible expression of what is intangible and recalls for the audience how "eternal life" was "promised before eternal ages" (1:2a–c) but concretely "revealed (ἐφανέρωσεν) at the proper time" (1:3). In the LXX the verb refers specifically to the manifestation of God's help or salvific favor and has eschatological tones of glory (e.g., Gen 35:7; Ps 30:17; Joel 3:4). In Greco-Roman religious and political discourse, it refers to the appearance of their gods, heroes, and emperors.[42] Thus, the audience understand that the present "grace" that Paul has prayed for on their behalf for empowerment is qualitatively similar to the helping and saving "grace of God" that has already "appeared,"

Titus 2:11b-12 (a')

The "grace of God" is further defined as "saving all human beings." The adjective "saving" (σωτήριος) highlights for the audience the saving nature of the appearance of God's grace. The first occurrence of ἄνθρωπος referred to unbelievers—"human beings (ἀνθρώπων) who turn away the truth" (1:14). Here too "human beings" (ἀνθρώποις) refers to unbelievers, but the modifier "all" (πᾶσιν) suggests to the audience that the apostle has in mind "all" types of unbelievers who are exposed to all types of Christians—older unbelieving men, older unbelieving women, younger unbelieving women, younger unbelieving men, and unbelieving masters.[43]

That the "grace of God" is not only a saving event in history but also an empowering event—as noted above—is shown further in 2:12 by the opening participial clause "training us" (παιδεύουσα ἡμᾶς). The participle "training" connotes "to assist in the development of a person's ability to make appropriate choices."[44] The pronoun "us" (ἡμᾶς) includes the apostle who shares in the "grace" from "God our (ἡμῶν) savior" (1:3) and "Christ Jesus our (ἡμῶν) savior" (1:4). The audience recognize, therefore, that the "grace of God" is not just a past event but also—as the present

---

42. See Towner, *Letters*, 745.

43. This conclusion is supported by noting how all other uses of the term ἄνθρωπος in the letter (1:14; 3:2, 8, 10) refer to unbelievers or troublemakers whose faith is questionable. In addition, when the apostle describes those who have been redeemed already, he use the term λαόν (2:14).

44. BDAG, s.v.

participle indicates—an immediate source of power for all the elect of God.

The purpose (ἵνα) of this "training" is that "we might live sensibly and righteously and godly in the present age." The verb "live" (ζήσωμεν) is the main verb of the purpose clause, which is modified immediately before and after by the participles "denying" (ἀρνησάμενοι) in 2:12 and "awaiting" (προσδεχόμενοι) in 2:13a. This "training" has made a new and empowered life possible; but the pursuit of this life "in the present" must be accompanied by denial of the past life and expectation of the future life.

The denial of the former life is indicated by the first participial statement "denying ungodliness and worldly desires." The participle "denying" (ἀρνησάμενοι) recalls for the audience the opposition who "profess to know [God] but by their works they deny (ἀρνοῦνται)" (1:16). Its occurrence in 2:12 connotes a complete turnabout—a personal and intentional rejection of one lifestyle for another; thus, the audience perceive that the act of denial is much more than a contradiction of facts. The present tense of the participle "denying" reminds the audience that their present lives must be characterized by a constant denial of their former way of existence and its corollary pursuits.

Various forms of "ungodliness" (ἀσέβειαν) occur in the LXX to describe the wicked (e.g., Exod 9:27; Ps 1:1). The term recalls for the audience the earlier occurrence of "godliness" (1:1a), given the two differ only in their prefixes (ἀσέβειαν/εὐσέβειαν); thus "ungodliness" is understood as the antithesis of "godliness"—the "lack of reverence for deity and hallowed institutions."[45] This vertical irreverence is expressed concretely in the pursuit of "worldly desires." "Desires" (ἐπιθυμίας) refers to inordinate "desires"—lusts—that are "worldly" (κοσμικάς) and transitory by nature. Having heard the cognate "to adorn" (κοσμέω), the audience understand these "desires" as cravings that are "adorable" or "appealing" in the eyes of the world. Being "worldly desires," they stand in contrast to the "hope of eternal life" (1:1a) that was promised before the creation of this world (1:2c) by the God who transcends this world and has graced the "elect of God" (1:1a) to participate in his divine mode of existence.

The "a'" sub-element concludes with a description of the present life itself: "we might live sensibly and righteously and godly in the pres-

45. BDAG, s.v.

ent age." Cognates of the three adverbs "sensibly" (σωφρόνως), "righteously" (δικαίως), and "godly" (εὐσεβῶς) occurred earlier in the letter to describe Christian conduct. The elder, for instance, must be "sensible" (σώφρονα, 1:8; see also 2:2, 4, 5, 6) and "just" (δίκαιον, 1:8). The "faith of the elect of God" is their "recognition of the truth according to godliness (εὐσέβειαν)" (1:1b). Now, however, it becomes explicit to the audience that these qualities characterize the new lifestyle required of all believers as a result of the appearance of the "grace of God." Given this grace and the eternal life that is now theirs through faith in Christ, the audience are to "live sensibly and righteously and godly in the present age."

The plural form of ζήσωμεν reminds the audience that the pursuit of this new life is a communal pursuit, realized particularly when the elder "exhorts with sound doctrine and reproves those who oppose" (1:9b); when the "older women . . . make sensible the younger women" (2:3–5); and when Titus and—implicitly—the "older men" present themselves as "model[s] of commendable works" for the "younger men" (2:6–8). The audience thus realize that living "sensibly and righteously and godly" requires continual mutual exhortation and reproof from different members of their community.

The noun "age" (αἰῶνι) recalls for the audience that God promised "eternal life" (1:2a) "before eternal (αἰωνίων) ages" (1:2c). The audience thus have a rich worldview that interconnects life "in the present age" with the preceding and proceeding ages, all of which center on the "hope of eternal life": "eternal life" was promised "before eternal ages"; it has been revealed partially "in the present age" through the appearance of the "grace of God"; and it will be realized fully in the coming age when Christ returns. Like Paul, then, who is a "slave of God and apostle of Jesus Christ . . . on the basis of the hope of eternal life" (1:1a-b), the audience are to live commendably according to this hope by pursuing sensibility, righteousness, and godliness.

4. Titus 2:13a (D): Awaiting the Blessed Hope

Life "in the present age" is modified further in the D element, the pivot of the microchiasm, in terms of "awaiting the blessed hope." The translation "awaiting" (προσδεχόμενοι) aptly captures the sense of eager and confident expectation. The reason why the audience can await with confidence is because God cannot lie (1:2b). For the audience, then, life "in the present age" involves both "denying ungodliness and worldly desires" in view of the past work of "God our savior" and "awaiting the blessed hope" in view of the future work of "God our savior." The apostle's explicit reference to the "hope of eternal life" (1:2a) at the outset of the letter, however, suggests to the audience that "awaiting the blessed hope" should have some prominence in their thinking.

The object of the participle "awaiting" is the "blessed hope." "Hope" reminds the audience of the basis for Paul's apostolic faithfulness—the "hope (ἐλπίδι) of eternal life" (1:2a). The adjective "blessed" (μακαρίαν) carries the nuance of "privileged." In Greco-Roman literature the adjective refers to "one on whom fortune smiles."[46] Similarly, in the LXX it refers to divine favor (e.g., Deut 33:29; Ps 31:1; Isa 30:18). In this letter these ideas of fortune and divine favor are reflected in Paul's own gracious call as a "slave of God and apostle of Jesus Christ" and in the audience's gracious election (1:1a). The hope that Paul and the audience have, then, is a "blessed" or "privileged" hope because it is a hope exclusively for those who have been called by God. For this reason the phrase "blessed hope" challenges the audience to live apart from the Cretan culture on account of their privileged status.[47]

5. Titus 2:13b (C'): Redeemed for Commendable Works

In the C' element of the third macrochiasm, the apostle expands on what the "blessed hope" entails: "the appearance of the glory of our great God and savior Jesus Christ."[48] The noun "appearance" (ἐπιφάνειαν) echoes the earlier epiphany language of 1:3 (ἐφανέρωσεν) and 2:11 (ἐπιφάνη). Similar to its verbal cognate in 2:11, "appearance" evokes notions of God's intervention to bring help and salvation. The repetitive language connects for the audience the future "appearance" with the past "appearance," creating a distinct Christian worldview according to which the audience are to "live sensibly and righteously and godly" (2:12).[49]

---

46. BDAG, s.v.

47. For a more extended discussion of the theme "blessed hope," see Ladd, *The Blessed Hope*, 137–61.

48. The καί between "hope" and "appearance" is epexegetical and has, therefore, been excluded from the translation to clarify its purpose.

49. See Matera, *New Testament Theology*, 243–45.

Paul describes the future epiphany in terms of "the glory of our great God and savior Jesus Christ."[50] In the LXX the term "glory" refers frequently to divine power that is materialized in tangible but awe-inspiring ways. Also, the "glory of the Lord" is depicted as something distinct from its appearance (e.g., Exod 24:17). Thus, the apostle is likely expressing the "appearance of the glory" versus "the glorious appearance." Similarly, "glory" is distinct from "our great God and savior Jesus Christ" rather than in apposition with "Jesus Christ." The most compelling reason for this is that 2:13b is parallel to 2:11, which speaks about the "appearance" of the "grace of God" more as an event than as a person. The audience, therefore, are to view the second appearance not only as the climactic return of the person of Christ but also as the revelation of his "glory" which the "elect" will participate in.

According to the Granville Sharp rule, when two nouns are singular, personal, and common (not proper names) they have the same reference.[51] Thus, the phrase τοῦ μεγάλου θεοῦ καὶ σωτῆρος ἡμῶν Ἰησοῦ Χριστοῦ is a reference to one person—"Jesus Christ." That "God and savior" was a common title both in Jewish and Greco-Roman literature to denote a single deity supports further that the audience hear the phrase

50. The different translations for this phrase reflect the host of exegetical questions surrounding it. A comparison of just the *NAB*, *ESV*, and *NET* illustrates the point:
NAB: the appearance of the glory of the great God and of our savior Jesus Christ
ESV: the appearing of the glory of our great God and Savior Jesus Christ
NET: the glorious appearing of our great God and Savior, Jesus Christ
Several observations regarding the differences between the translations will highlight some of the relevant exegetical questions at hand. First, the *NET* understands the genitive "of glory" as a Hebraic expression of "glorious"; hence, "the glorious appearing. . . ." The *NAB* and *ESV*, however, give a wooden but straightforward translation of the Greek. "Glory," then, does not modify "appearing" but stands as a distinct entity. Second, by repeating the preposition "of" before "the great God" and "our savior Jesus Christ" the *NAB* suggests two distinct persons, whereas the *ESV* and *NET* understand the apostle as referring solely to one person ("Jesus Christ"). Third, the comma before "Jesus Christ" in the *NET* is not insignificant; it suggests that "Jesus Christ" is appositional to "glorious appearing" or "glory," whereas the *ESV* suggests that "Jesus Christ" is appositional to "our great God and Savior." "Glory," then, is to be understood as belonging to or coming from "Jesus Christ" rather than being "Jesus Christ" himself. For a more detailed discussion of the challenges surrounding the interpretation of this phrase, see Mounce, *Pastoral Epistles*, 426–31; Marshall, *Pastoral Epistles*, 274–96; Bowman, "Jesus Christ, God Manifest," 733–52.

51. For additional comments on Sharp's rule, see Wallace, *Greek Grammar*, 270–78; BDF §276; Harris, *Jesus as God: The New Testament Use of Theos in Reference to Jesus*, 173–85.

as a reference to a single person.[52] The "glory" in view, then, is referring specifically to the glory of "our great God and savior Jesus Christ." Given that during this time the emperor adopted the title "savior" freely, this exaltation of Christ as "savior" challenges the audience to view Christ alone as the divine "savior."[53]

The phrase, however, appears intentionally ambiguous in order to make a subtle claim about the divinity of Christ. Several observations illustrate the point. First, while the apostle distinguishes between "God" and "Jesus Christ" in the description of his calling (1:1a), the lines are less clear immediately after. In 1:3 he states that he was "considered faithful according to the command of God our savior (σωτῆρος ἡμῶν θεοῦ)"—which echoes references to "God" in 1:1a and 1:2, but in 1:4 he describes "Christ Jesus" also as "our savior" (σωτῆρος ἡμῶν). Given the proximity of the verses the audience notice the correlation between the two persons who are both referred to as "savior." Second, the phrase "God our savior" (σωτῆρος ἡμῶν θεοῦ) in 2:10b is the exact phrase found in 1:3, but it occurs in the C element (2:10b-12) of the third microchiasm (1:13b–3:3), which is parallel to the C' element (2:14–15a), thus suggesting that "our great God and savior" refers to God the Father. "Jesus Christ" would then be appositional to "glory." Finally, the adjective "great" (μεγάλου) occurs regularly in the LXX as an appellation for God (e.g., Exod 18:11; 1 Chr 16:25; Ps 94:3). Therefore, while the audience understand the expression as a reference to a single person, they experience the subtle manner in which Paul affirms the deity of Christ.

Titus 2:14–15a (B'): Redemption and Cleansing through Jesus Christ

In Titus 2:14–15a the audience hear the B' element of the third chiastic unit (1:13b–3:3) as a mini-chiasm in itself. Verses 14–15a are composed carefully of three sub-elements:

a. [14a] who gave himself (ἑαυτόν) on behalf of us,

b. [14b] so that he might redeem us from all lawlessness

a'. [14c] and cleanse for himself (ἑαυτῷ) a special people, zealous for commendable works.

[15a] These things speak and exhort

52. See Harris, *Jesus as God*, 178–79; Towner, *Letters*, 756.

53. See Wright, "Paul's Gospel and Caesar's Empire," 160–83; Smith and Song, "Some Christological Implications in Titus 2:13," 284–94; Murray J. Harris, "Titus 2:13 and the Deity of Christ," 262–77.

This mini-chiasm coheres around the work of Christ—what he did (2:14a) and why (2:14b-c). The repetition of the pronoun "himself"—"gave himself (ἑαυτόν)" in 2:14a and "cleanse for himself (ἑαυτῷ)" in 2:14c—establishes the parallelism between the two sub-elements. This term does not occur anywhere else in the letter.

Titus 2:14a (a)

The mini-chiasm begins with the relative clause "who gave himself on behalf of us." The clause highlights the sacrificial and representative nature of Christ's death. The sacrificial nature of Christ's death is evidenced by both the subject and active voice of the verb "gave" (ἔδωκεν).[54] After expressions of suffering, dying, or sacrifice, the preposition ὑπέρ expresses "on behalf of."[55] Thus the relative clause highlights for the audience the *substitutionary* nature of Christ's death: he died for their sake. In addition, the pronoun "us" (ἡμῶν) communicates that the death of Christ is not only *substitutionary but also uniting.*

Titus 2:14b (b)

In the pivot of the mini-chiasm the apostle states the negative purpose (ἵνα) for why Christ "gave himself": "so that he might redeem us from all lawlessness." Literally the verb "redeem" (λυτρώσηται) means "to free by paying a ransom"; figuratively the verb means "to liberate from an oppressive situation"[56] and occurs frequently in the LXX as a designation for the Lord, undoubtedly recalling in particular the exodus account (e.g., Exod 6:6; Ps 18:15; Zech 10:8). The verb described the practice of buying a slave's or prisoner's freedom by paying a ransom; thus it would have resonated with the Christian "slaves" (2:9–10a) and enhanced the audience's understanding of why the apostle refers to himself now as a "slave of God" (1:1a). That Paul applies it, however, to all of "us" causes the audience to recognize their common spiritual plight: apart from the "grace of God" all of them were in slavery and in need of redemption. Despite their different status as "older men" and "older women," "younger women" and "younger

---

54. The Father as subject (see John 3:16) or the passive voice ("was given") would have lessened the apostle's emphasis that Christ, according to his own volition, "gave *himself* (ἑαυτόν)."

55. BDAG, s.v.

56. BDAG, s.v.

men," "slaves" or freemen, prior to the "grace of God" all of them were enslaved.

Continuing with his remarks on redemption, Paul specifies that Christ "redeemed us from all lawlessness (ἀπὸ πάσης ἀνομίας)." A similar expression is found in Ps 129:8: "And he himself will redeem (λυτρώσεται) Israel from all his iniquities (πασῶν τῶν ἀνομιῶν αὐτοῦ)." The similarities suggest that Paul is borrowing the psalmist's language.[57] The substitution of "Israel" with "us" in 2:14 communicates to the audience the apostle's understanding of the new Israel. The term "lawlessness" is used in the LXX to describe generally those who oppose God and specifically those who violate his requirements for holiness from Israel (e.g., Lev 20:14; Ps 35:4). The adjective "all" (πάσης) communicates to the audience that they have been redeemed from "lawlessness" itself. The preposition "from" (ἀπό), therefore, indicates that Christ's death has removed the "elect of God" (1:1b) from the "sphere" or "power" of "lawlessness."[58] Recognizing the similarity between their enslavement to "lawlessness" and Israel's enslavement to Pharaoh in Egypt, the audience understand now why it was necessary for God to "appear" again in a much more powerful way through Christ Jesus. The statement that Christ has "redeemed us from all (πάντα) lawlessness" also reinforces the audience's grasp of their identity as the "clean" for whom "all things (πάντα) are clean" (1:15) and their new ability to do "every (πᾶν) good work" (1:16).

Titus 2:14c–15a (a')

In the "a'" sub-element Paul states the positive purpose for Christ's self-sacrifice: to "cleanse for himself a special people, zealous for commendable works." The verb "cleanse" (καθαρίσῃ) recalls for the audience Paul's earlier statement: "All things are clean (καθαρά) to the clean (καθαροῖς). But to the defiled and unfaithful nothing is clean (καθαρόν)" (1:15). Like its cognate noun, the verb refers to inner spiritual purity, a condition of being free from moral guilt. According to the "a" and "b" sub-elements the redemption in view involved Christ giving "himself" (2:14a) to "redeem us" from a sphere or power of "lawlessness" (2:14b). Thus the audience perceive that the cleansing in view refers similarly to an inner spiritual renewal involving redemption from the sphere of "lawlessness."

57. For possible other OT connections with ransom language, see Edwards, "Reading the Ransom Logion in 1 Tim 2,6 and Titus 2,14 with Isa 42,6–7; 49,6–8," 264–66.

58. See Witherington, *Letters*, 145.

Moreover, it is now explicit that their state of being "clean" (1:15) is a direct consequence of Christ's self-sacrifice, a work of grace.

The language "for himself a special people" has strong echoes of Ezek 37:23: "That they may no longer defile themselves (μιαίνωνται) in their idols; and I will deliver them from all their lawlessness (ἀνομιῶν) in which they have sinned, and I will cleanse (καθαριῶ) them; and they will be to me a people (λαόν), and I will be to them God." What is noteworthy about this OT text is its use of covenant language: "they will be to me a people, and I will be to them God." Similarly, in Titus 2:14 the apostle highlights how Christ "gave himself on behalf of us, so that he might redeem us from all lawlessness (ἀνομίας) and cleanse (καθαρίσῃ) for himself a special people (λαόν)"; in short, Christ's self-sacrifice (ἑαυτόν) for a people was for the purpose of forming for himself (ἑαυτῷ) a people. Paul thus applies the two related themes of purification and election from Ezek 37:23 to highlight that he, Titus, and the Cretan community, have entered into a covenant relationship with Christ and thus have become a "special people" who belong to Christ. Indeed, the use of the phrase "special people" (λαὸν περιούσιον)—commonly used in the LXX to highlight Israel's status as an elect and exalted people (e.g., Exod 19:5; Deut 7:6; 14:2)—reiterates the audience's new privileged status.

The adjective "zealous" expresses "earnest commitment" and occurs regularly in the LXX to describe either God's zeal for his own glory or devotion to God and Torah (e.g., Deut 4:23–24; Exod 34:14; 1 Macc 2:24). The phrase "commendable works" (καλῶν ἔργων) recalls for the audience Paul's specific exhortation to Titus to be a "model of commendable works (καλῶν ἔργων)" (2:7b). The repetition indicates for the audience that Titus is not only a "model" for the "younger men" (2:6–8) but also for the entire audience. Being "cleansed," the audience are now not only qualified "for all good work" (1:16) but should also be "zealous for commendable works." Finally, this concluding phrase to the brief doctrinal excursus ties the apostle's theological instruction (2:11–14) to the preceding ethical teaching (2:1–10), "ensuring the close relationship between theology (as anchored in the historical Christ-event) and ethics (the life that this event 'teaches'; 2:12)."[59] In this regard he demonstrates for the audience—but especially for the elder who is to "exhort with sound doctrine

59. Towner, *Letters*, 764.

and reprove" (1:9b)—that exhortation and reproof are to be done according to sound doctrine—specifically according to the hope of eternal life.

Bringing this mini-chiasm to a close, Paul—recalling the verbs "speak" (λάλει) in 2:1 and "exhort" (παρακάλει) in 2:6—commands in a summary fashion: "These things speak and exhort. . . ." In the corresponding B element the audience heard, "Speak (λάλει) what is consistent with sound doctrine" (2:1). This general command was followed by specific exhortations to different members among the audience. In 2:15, however, the expression "these things" (ταῦτα) no longer pertains just to behavior that is "consistent with sound doctrine" but includes also the "doctrine of God our savior" itself.[60] The repetition of the commands to "speak" and "exhort" reinforces for the audience Paul's original concern for godly conduct, which spurred his reflections on its doctrinal basis. In addition it highlights both the complementary duties of Titus's role in instructing and exhorting and the audience's role in submitting and obeying.

Titus 2:15b–3:3 (A'): Living Submissively, Obediently, and Graciously

In the A' element of the third chiastic unit (1:13b–3:3) the audience hear 2:15b–3:2 as a mini-chiasm in itself. These verses are composed carefully of three sub-elements:

> a. [15b] and reprove with all (πάσης) command; no one (μηδείς) should disregard you.
>
>> b. [3:1] Remind them to submit to ruling authorities, to be obedient, to be ready for every good work,
>
> a'. [2] to blaspheme no one (μηδένα), to be unquarrelsome, considerate, demonstrating all (πᾶσαν) gentleness to all (πάντας) human beings.

This mini-chiasm continues the theme of new life in view of "the grace of God [that] has appeared" (2:11). The central role that Titus plays in exhorting and reproving the Cretan community continues also. In addition, while 2:2–10a focused on how the audience should conduct themselves with respect to one another, here the concern falls on the audience's relationship to those outside of the community of faith.[61] The verbs "reprove"

---

60. There is some disagreement regarding the extent of the reference. Mounce (*Pastoral Epistles*, 432), for instance, argues that the apostle is going as far back as 1:5. The repetition of "speak" (λάλει) in 2:1 and 2:15, however, limits the extent of the reference to 2:1. Quinn (*Letter*, 177) suggests that ταῦτα may have a forward reference as well.

61. See Witherington, *Letters*, 154.

(2:15b) and "remind" (3:1) suggest that Paul is addressing again the presence of "rebels, empty-talkers and deceivers" (1:10) and their influence over "whole households" (1:11).

Titus 2:15b (a)

In the first sub-element Paul commands Titus: "reprove with all command; let no one disregard you." Taken with the preceding verb "exhort" (παρακάλει, 2:15a) the verb "reprove" recalls for the audience the elder's basic calling to "exhort (παρακαλεῖν) with sound doctrine and reprove (ἐλέγχειν) those who oppose" (1:9b). It occurrence here indicates that the apostle is returning to the specific problem of troublemakers and his general concern for rebellious attitudes. At the same time the absence of a specific object in 2:15b, in contrast to the first two occurrences of the verb, suggests that the apostle has a broader audience in view: it is not only "those who oppose" (1:9b) who need to be reproved but also the audience—especially those who are paying attention to the false teachers (1:10–16).

The command to "reprove" is followed by the prepositional phrase "with all command"[62] and the command "let no one disregard you." The first phrase recalls for the audience Paul's own authority that is "according to the command (ἐπιταγήν) of God our savior" (1:3); Paul has authority because he is under God's authority. Similarly, Titus is to "reprove with all command (ἐπιταγῆς)," recognizing that he too has authority because he is under the apostle's authority. The apostle has underscored already Titus's authority by referring to him as a "true child according to a common faith" (1:4) and through the somewhat superfluous clause "as I directed you" at the end of 1:5. Now, through the adjective "all" (πάσης) this authority is further highlighted and strengthened. In addition, the repetition of the term "command," which occurs uniquely in 1:3 and 2:15b of the letter, suggests to the audience a more explicit reference to the divine quality of even Titus's authority: like Paul, Titus ministers "according to the command of God our savior."

That Titus should "reprove with all authority" is reiterated negatively through the exhortation, "let no one disregard you." The verb "disregard" connotes "to have disdain for" or "despise."[63] The pronoun "no one"

---

62. The first phrase might also modify the commands to "speak and exhort" (2:15a).
63. BDAG, s.v.

(μηδείς) includes not only the opposition—the "rebels, empty-talkers and deceivers" (1:10)—but also all who belong to the household of God (2:1–10a). For Titus and all the future elders, the negative command indicates that they must not let allow anyone to disregard their exhortations and reproofs. For the audience this closing phrase has a double force: individually they are to respect Titus and corporately they are to exhort and reprove one another to do likewise: "let no one disregard" him.[64]

Titus 3:1 (b)

In the "b" sub-element, the pivot of the mini-chiasm, Paul begins a new imperative: "Remind them to submit to ruling authorities, to be obedient, to be ready for all good work." The verb "remind" (ὑπομίμνῃσκε) indicates that the audience have already been instructed in the exhortations that follow. The verb also suggests that some audience members have forgotten these exhortations perhaps by "paying attention to Jewish myths and regulations of human beings who turn away the truth" (1:14).

Although many translations distinguish the two nouns ἀρχαῖς and ἐξουσίαις as different levels of authority (e.g., *NAB, ESV*), the earliest and best witnesses lack the conjunction kai,. Therefore, the two nouns should be taken together ("ruling authorities") as a general description of all official powers.[65] The audience (αὐτούς) are reminded "to submit" (ὑποτάσσεσθαι)" to all who have legitimate authority.[66] This reminder is especially relevant given Cretans were notorious for their rebellion against all outside authority.[67] Moreover, the juxtaposition of the command to submit to those in authority with the command to exhort with all authority—in addition to the earlier references to authority (e.g., Paul's apostolic authority in 1:1–4)—communicates to the audience Paul's overarching concern in the letter for acknowledging and respecting legitimate authority.

This third occurrence of "submit" progresses the audience's understanding of submission. According to 2:5 the "younger women" are to

64. For additional reflections on the rhetorical function of the expression, "no one should disregard you," see Wendland, "Let No One Disregard You," 334–51.

65. Collins (*Titus*, 357) translates the phrase as "legitimate rulers."

66. Commentators do not agree over which group the pronoun αὐτούς refers to. The absence of an antecedent, however, suggests that the same extensive group from 2:1–15b is in view.

67. See Kelly, *Pastoral Epistles*, 249.

"submit (ὑποτασσομένας) to their own husbands." Similarly slaves are to "submit (ὑποτάσσεσθαι) to their own masters" (2:9). In both instances the term describes a disposition appropriate to existing structures and expressed concretely in various ways. This third occurrence describes also a proper posture, and it too is defined concretely in terms of attitude and actions. However, the audience understand better that submissiveness is a quality that should characterize all believers, stemming from a recognition and acceptance of different structures which God has established.[68] Being redeemed (2:14), therefore, does not mean that the audience are free to live however they please. Rather, recognizing God's sovereignty, which was manifested in election and revelation (1:1–3), the audience are to "submit to ruling authorities." By adopting this appropriate disposition the audience distinguish themselves from the "rebels" (1:10) who disregard apostolic authority and teaching.

The verb "to be obedient" (πειθαρχεῖν) describes the normal practice of good citizens and generally refers to obedience to laws. The absence of further specification communicates to the audience that while submission to "ruling authorities" should be expressed concretely (e.g., paying taxes), the apostle is more concerned about a general attitude of obedience. Again, it is clear that he has in mind a contrast with those who are "disobedient" (ἀπειθεῖς, 1:16).

The phrase "to be ready for all good work" (πρὸς πᾶν ἔργον ἀγαθὸν ἑτοίμους εἶναι)[69] echoes both Paul's description in 1:16 of those who are "unqualified for all good work (πρὸς πᾶν ἔργον ἀγαθὸν ἀδόκιμοι)" and language used in Greco-Roman literature to describe wealthy citizens who made financial contributions to the city-states in exchange for recognition and praise.[70] In contrast to those who are "unqualified for all

68. See Wainwright, "Praying for Kings," 122.

69. Sometimes the apostle uses the adjective καλός (2:7b, 14; 3:8, 14) with "works" and other times ἀγαθός (1:16; 3:1). Whether the apostle is trying to bring out a particular nuance is difficult to discern. Nevertheless, whenever he addresses the topic of obedience and submission in the letter, he uses the latter (1:16; 2:5, 10; 3:1). It appears that the apostle uses the adjective when he is describing work that is done out of submission to appropriate authorities. Thus, in 1:16 the "defiled" are "unqualified for all good work (ἔργον ἀγαθόν)" because they are "disobedient" (ἀπειθεῖς). In 2:5 the "younger women" are to be "good" (ἀγαθάς) as they submit to their husbands. In 2:9–10 slaves are to "demonstrate that in all respects faith is good (ἀγαθήν)" as they submit to their masters. The audience, then, in 3:1 are "to be ready for all 'good (ἀγαθόν) work'" as an outworking of their submission and obedience to "ruling authorities."

70. See Winter, Seek the Welfare of the City.

good work," the audience, who are the "special people, zealous for commendable works" (2:14), are to become the new model citizens for the city-states by being "ready for all good work."[71] The message to the audience is to be set apart by their "good works" in order to be noticed by their surrounding world. The false teachers, who embody the worst of Cretan vices (1:12), blend easily into the Cretan world and, in this way, give no indication that they have been uniquely redeemed and cleansed by God to be "for himself a special people" (2:14). The audience, however, are to make visible their presence in their immediate world by being "ready for all good work."

Titus 3:2 (a')

In the last sub-element of this mini-chiasm Paul explicates further what Titus is to remind the audience of. First, the audience are "to blaspheme (βλασφημεῖν) no one." The pronoun "no one" (μηδένα) marks a shift towards a more general audience ("all human beings") versus just the "ruling authorities." Just as "no one (μηδείς) should disregard" Titus (2:15b), so too the audience are to "blaspheme no one." Recalling the apostle's concern that "the word of God may not be blasphemed (βλασφημῆται)" (2:5), the audience recognize that they too are not to speak slanderously or insultingly about anyone. The correlation that is suggested by the repetition of the verb "blaspheme," which occurs uniquely in 2:5 and 3:2, between the "word of God" and "no one" must have been jarring to the audience. To guard the reputation of the "word of God" makes sense; but to guard the name and reputation of an ordinary citizen comes as a challenge, given "Cretans are always liars" (1:12). Although the apostle makes a clear distinction between the elect and nonelect, he exhibits a profound respect for all authority and all people. Lest the previous section (2:2–10a) leave the audience with the notion that believers are to care for only one another, Paul highlights that they are "to blaspheme no one."

In addition the audience "are to be unquarrelsome" (ἀμάχους εἶναι). The related noun μάχη and verb μάχομαι denote quarrels—"battles fought without actual weapons."[72] The adjective "unquarrelsome" reminds the audience of the elder who must not be "irritable" and "belligerent" and is a quality notably absent among the false teachers whose

71. See Towner, *Letters*, 770.
72. BDAG, s.v.

words are creating divisions among the audience. "To be unquarrelsome," then, is to adopt a lifestyle that is not unduly argumentative and offensive. This quality is especially noteworthy given the letter's emphasis on exhorting "with sound doctrine" (1:9b) and speaking "what is consistent with sound doctrine" (2:1): "holding fast to the faithful word" (1:9a) is not tantamount to being quarrelsome and belligerent. The audience must also remember to be "kind" (ἐπιεικεῖς). This adjective occurs in the LXX in the context of God's goodness and mercy (e.g., Ps 85:5; Dan 3:42). In view of the kindness that has been shown to them through the appearance of "the grace of God" (2:11), the audience are to be "kind" to believers and unbelievers alike.

Finally, the audience must be committed to "demonstrating all gentleness to all human beings." "Gentleness" (πραΰτητα) signifies a commitment to meekness versus force[73] and comes from "not being overly impressed by a sense of one's self-importance."[74] Cognizant of and committed to the grand scheme of salvation (1:1b–3), the audience should not be overwhelmed by a sense of self-importance. The participle "demonstrating" (ἐνδεικνυμένους) echoes the earlier exhortation to "slaves" to "demonstrate (ἐνδεικνυμένους) that in all respects faith is good" (2:10a). In both instances the term carries the nuance of validation—actions corroborating beliefs and words.[75] The implicit challenge to the audience is that not only is Titus worthy of imitation but also good Christian slaves: the latter's demonstration of humility and service towards their masters models the kind of gentleness and readiness to serve that the audience are to demonstrate to "all human beings."

The adjective "all" (πᾶσαν) communicates to the audience that "gentleness" must be demonstrated "completely"—consistently versus occasionally, fully instead of partially. The second occurrence of the adjective before "human beings" (ἀνθρώπους) functions as a rhetorical doublet: "Paul is urging 'all' gentleness to 'all' human beings."[76] Following the pattern of the "grace of God [that] has appeared, saving all human beings

---

73. Knight, *Pastoral Epistles*, 334: "It may be best understood by its contrast to its opposites, roughness, bad temper, sudden anger, and brusqueness."

74. BDAG, s.v.

75. Collins (*Titus*, 357) notes how the term originates from the world of rhetoric and is used here to highlight the appealing and persuasive impact that Christian conduct should have towards outsiders.

76. Knight, *Pastoral Epistles*, 334.

(πᾶσιν ἀνθρώποις)" (2:11), regardless of gender, ethnicity, or age, the audience are to demonstrate "gentleness" indiscriminately, impartially, and consistently.

Titus 3:3

To facilitate the exhortations given in 3:1–2, in 3:3 the apostle concludes the mini-chiasm by reminding the audience: "For we too were once ignorant, disobedient, misled, enslaved to various desires and pleasures, spending our lives in evil and envy, despicable, hating one another." The conjunction "for" (γάρ) indicates the link between what Paul just said in 3:1–2 and what follows. The personal pronoun "we" (ἡμεῖς), taken with the adverb "once" (ποτε), reminds the audience that the "elect of God" (1:1a)—the apostle, Titus, the Cretan members, and all other believers— in distinction to "all human beings" (3:2) were "once" like "all human beings": prior to the appearance of Jesus Christ, "who gave himself on behalf of us (ἡμῶν), so that he might redeem us (ἡμᾶς) from all lawlessness and cleanse for himself a special people" (2:14), "we too (καί)" were no different from "all human beings." The apostle's focus on the former life communicates to the audience that while they are to live in anticipation of "eternal life" (1:2a), they are not to forget that they too were "once" foolish, enslaved, and despicable. Remembering this reality guards them from the pride that could arise from misunderstanding the grace behind their elect status.

The first three adjectives ("ignorant, disobedient, misled") focus on living in ignorance. "Ignorant" (ἀνόητοι) can describe a simpleton or uneducated person, but its occurrences in the LXX (e.g., Deut 32:31; Ps 48:13; Prov 15:21) and the context of the letter suggest that the adjective refers specifically to ignorance of God and his power and promises. Prior to the revelation of God's word in the apostle's "proclamation" (1:3), the audience were "ignorant" of the "hope of eternal life" (1:2a).

The adjective "disobedient" (ἀπειθεῖς) is especially grating for the audience because it expresses one of the main deficiencies of "the defiled and unfaithful" (1:15) who are "vile and disobedient (ἀπειθεῖς) and un- qualified for all good work" (1:16). The audience perceive a clear contrast between this particular shortcoming and the reminder "to be obedient" (πειθαρχεῖν) to "ruling authorities" (3:1). Any continual disobedience, then, whether to Paul, Titus, or the "ruling authorities," signals to the audience that they themselves—like the false teacher—are still living according to the former existence outside of the revelation of God. The apostle's statement, "For we too were once . . . disobedient," is also ironic because it acknowledges that he "too" was "once" like the very ones he condemns in the letter. At the same time that the false teachers are described as "disobedient" communicates to the audience that they are not living according to the schema of the twofold epiphanies of the grace and power of God (2:10b–13).

Finally, the participle "misled" (πλανώμενοι) indicates being led from the proper direction or right way.[77] Again it is an apt descriptive reminder of the false teachers who go astray to "Jewish myths" and "who turn away the "truth" (1:14). Being "misled," these opponents are "upsetting whole households, teaching what is not necessary" (1:11). Thus, they are both deceived and deceiving others. Moreover, it is an apt description of all humanity who are without God's revelation and thus taught to live according to false promises.

The next phrase indicates that "we too were once . . . enslaved to various desires and pleasures." "Desires" (ἐπιθυμίαις) recalls for the audience the phrase "worldly desires (ἐπιθυμίας)" (2:12), which the audience are to deny in view of the "grace of God [that] has appeared" (2:11). The audience now perceive that they are called to deny what once had mastery over them. While the term "pleasures" (ἡδοναῖς) refers occasionally in Greco-Roman literature to good desires, it usually carries a negative sense, connoting an evil pleasure or illicit desire (e.g., Plutarch Per. 11.4; Xenophon Hell. 4.8.22).[78] The participle "enslaved" (δουλεύοντες) reiterates to the audience one of the apostle's core convictions: everyone is "enslaved" to someone or something. The "older women" in the audience are not to be "enslaved (δεδουλωμένας) to much wine" (2:3). Paul himself defines his present identity in terms of being a "slave (δοῦλος) of God" (1:1a). Redemption through "Jesus Christ," then, is not a shift from enslavement to freedom but a transference from one rule to another. Specifically, it is a transference from being "enslaved to various desires and pleasures" to being "enslaved" to God as a "special people, zealous for commendable works" (2:14). For this reason even "slaves" (δούλους) who "submit to their own masters in all things" (2:10a) do so out of their

77. BDAG, s.v.
78. BDAG, s.v.

allegiance to Christ—"that they might adorn the doctrine of God our savior" (2:10b). The audience recognize, therefore, that persisting in "various desires and pleasures" instead of "denying ungodliness and worldly desires" represents an implicit rejection of Christ's lordship and continual enslavement to "worldly desires."

Finally, the apostle describes their former existence in terms of antisocial behavior: "spending our lives in evil and envy, despicable, hating one another." The sequence of the final statement suggests a movement from evil thoughts to outward hatred. The preposition "in" (ἐν) expresses a sphere or domain of existence. This idea is reinforced by the participle "spending lives" (διάγοντες), which describes a way of life.[79] In such vice lists the noun "evil" (κακία|) refers to a "mean-spirited or vicious attitude."[80] In the first half of this final statement, then, Paul depicts the general mindset of their former lives that expressed itself naturally in blasphemy, irritability, spite, and bitterness. In other words, formerly their fallen mindset resulted in a life contrary to what the apostle calls them to in 3:1–2. Instead of being "ready for all good (ἀγαθόν) work," they lived in "evil"; instead of "blaspheming no one . . . [and] demonstrating all gentleness to all human beings," they lived in "envy" (φθόνῳ).

The closing words "despicable, hating others" express tangibly the result of "spending our lives in evil and envy." "Evil" persons are naturally "despicable" (στυγητοί)—that is, hated by others.[81] "Envy" leads to hatred for those who have what one lacks. The combination of malice and hatred towards others will naturally be met by hatred, resulting in a society of "hating others" (μισοῦντες ἀλλήλους).[82] That Paul states "we too were once . . ." highlights that no one is to view himself solely as the recipient of "evil and hatred." Rather, everyone is equally guilty of being the subject of malice and jealousy. Given this reality that everyone is both a perpetrator and victim of "evil and envy," the audience appreciate more deeply how the appearance of the "grace of God" broke this vicious cycle. Apart from this divine intervention the world would have continued in its downward spiral of mutual hatred.

---

79. See Epictetus *Discourses* 4.11.

80. BDAG, s.v.

81. The term can also mean "hateful." Compare *1 Clem* 35:6 ("hated") with 45:7 ("hateful"), but the citations in BDAG lean towards the passive sense.

82. See BDAG, s.v., for the notion of reciprocity inherent in the term ἀλλήλους.

SUMMARY OF CHAPTER FIVE

1. The theme "Exhort and Reprove to Commendable Works accord-
    ing to the Hope of Eternal Life" is explicit in the third microchiasm
    (1:13b—3:3). According to the A element (1:13b–16) Titus must
    "reprove" (1:13b) the false teachers (1:10–13a) severely. The salient
    characteristic of these "human beings who turn away the truth" is
    their hypocrisy: "They profess to know [God] but by their works
    they deny" (1:16). According to the B element (2:1–10a)—in con-
    trast to the false teachers who are "teaching what is not necessary"
    (1:11)—Titus is to turn the Cretan community towards the truth by
    speaking "what is consistent with sound doctrine" (2:1). According
    to the C (2:10b–12) and C' (2:13b) elements the "doctrine of God
    our savior" (2:10b) is bracketed by two appearances—the appear-
    ance of the "grace of God" (2:11) and the "appearance of the glory
    of our great God and savior Jesus Christ" (2:13b). According to the
    D element (2:13a), the pivot of the microchiasm, the pursuit of sen-
    sible, just, and godly lives "in the present age" involves not only the
    denial of "ungodliness and worldly desires" (2:12) but also—and
    especially—the anticipation of the "blessed hope" (2:13a). This is
    the "hope of eternal life" (1:2a) that the apostle referred to in the
    opening of the letter. According to the B' element (2:14–15a) Titus
    is commanded again to "speak and exhort" (2:15a) according to
    sound doctrine, doctrine that highlights the redemption, renewal,
    and calling to live commendably that have come in and through
    Jesus Christ. Finally, in the A' element—in view of the presence and
    influence of false teachers—Titus is to "reprove with all command,"
    reminding the audience of their calling to live in the eyes of "all
    human beings" differently from their former lives of ignorance,
    enslavement, and hatred.

2. The third microchiasm (1:13b—3:3) consists of seven elements
    and progresses the theme "Exhort and Reprove to Commendable
    Works according to the Hope of Eternal Life."

3. In the opening A element (1:13b–16) of the chiasm Paul commands
    Titus to "reprove" the opponents "severely," condemning them as
    "vile and disobedient and unqualified for all good work" (1:16).
    By doing so Paul continues to exercise his apostleship through

Titus. Recognizing the influence of these false teachers "who are upsetting whole households" (1:11) and his own duty as a "true child according to a common faith" (1:4), Titus is to "reprove" the opponents with the same severity that Paul exhibits towards them in this element. Recognizing Paul's apostolic authority, the Cretan community must stop "paying attention to Jewish myths and regulations of human beings who turn away the truth" (1:14) and dismiss the false teachers as "unqualified for all good work" (1:16).

4. In the B element (2:1–10a) the audience perceive a special emphasis on conduct that "is consistent with sound doctrine" (2:1). Through Titus's exhortations they experience further Paul's apostolic ministry that is "according to the faith of the elect of God" (1:1a)—their "recognition of the truth according to godliness" (1:1b). By living sensibly and exhorting and reproving one another—through word and example—to do likewise, the audience demonstrate the sincerity of their faith, unlike the opponents who "profess to know [God] but by their works they deny" (1:16). Moreover, in Titus they see a model elder who speaks and exhorts "what is consistent with sound doctrine" in contrast to the "rebels, empty-talkers and deceivers" who are "teaching what is not necessary" (1:10–11), and who presents himself as a "model of commendable works" (2:7b) in contrast to the "defiled and unfaithful" who are "unqualified for all good work" (1:15–16). Consequently, the audience are to recognize Titus's leadership and reject the authority and teaching of "those who oppose" (1:9b).

5. In the C (2:10b–12) and C' (2:13b) elements and in the D element (2:13a), the pivot of the microchiasm, the apostle reiterates the inseparable link between "recognition of the truth" and "godliness" (1:1b). The audience are reminded that the pursuit of "godliness" in the present age is bracketed by the "grace of God [that] has appeared" (2:11) and the "appearance of the glory of our great God and savior Jesus Christ" (2:13b). They are also reminded that just as Paul ministers as a "slave of God and apostle of Jesus Christ" (1:1a) "on the basis of the hope of eternal life" (1:2a), so too the audience are to "live sensibly and righteously and godly in the present age" (2:12) "awaiting the blessed hope" (2:13a).

6. In the B' element (2:14–15a) Paul specifies the twofold purpose of Christ's sacrifice—to "redeem us from all lawlessness and cleanse for himself a special people, zealous for commendable works" (2:14)—and thus progresses the audience's understanding of why "recognition of the truth" is "according to godliness" (1:1b). Specifically, the audience recognize better the christological basis for living commendably according to 2:2–10a. Moreover, the repeated command to Titus, "These things speak and exhort" (2:15a), reinforces not only Titus's obligation to "Exhort and Reprove to Commendable Works according to the Hope of Eternal Life" but also the need on the part of the Cretan community to take seriously Titus's words.

7. In the A' final element (2:15b—3:3) of the microchiasm Paul commands Titus to "reprove with all command" (2:15b), especially with respect to the audience's conduct towards those outside the "common faith" (1:4). The audience are to esteem Titus and reprove those who "disregard him." Moreover, recognizing that prior to the appearance of God's grace their lives were characterized by ignorance, enslavement, and hostility, they are to live differently now by submitting to "ruling authorities" (3:1) and by "demonstrating all gentleness to all human beings" (3:2).

6

Titus 3:4–15: Justified by Grace in Faith according to the Hope of Eternal Life (B')

A. [4] But when the kindness and the *love-for-human-beings* of God our savior appeared, [5] not from *works* that we did in righteousness; rather, according to his mercy he saved us through the washing of rebirth and renewal of the Holy Spirit, [6] whom he poured out on us richly through Jesus Christ our savior, [7] so that being made righteous by his *grace* we might become heirs according to the hope of eternal life. [8a] *Faithful* is the word, and about these things I want you to insist, so that *those who have faith in* God may be intent *to engage in commendable works*.

B. [8b] These are commendable and *useful* to *human beings*. [9a] But avoid foolish inquiries and genealogies and rivalries and quarrels about the *law*,

B'. [9b] for they are *useless* and empty. [10] After a first and second warning dismiss a heretical *human being*, [11] knowing that such a person is perverted and sinning, being self-decided. [12] When I send Artemas to you or Tychicus, hasten to come to me at Nicopolis, for I have decided to winter there. [13] Zenas the *lawyer* and Apollos hastily send, so that nothing is lacking for them.

A'. [14] And let also our own learn *to engage in commendable works* for urgent needs, so that they might not be unfruitful. [15] All who are with me greet you. Greet *those who love* us in the faith. *Grace* be with all of you.[1]

---

1. For the establishment of Titus 3:4–15 as a chiasm, see ch. 2.

CHIASTIC DEVELOPMENT
FROM TITUS 1:1–4 (A) TO 3:4–15 (A')

With Titus 3:4–15, the A' unit that brings to a climactic close the macro-chiastic structure of Titus, the audience hear echoes of Titus 1:1–4, the corresponding A unit that begins the macrochiasm. The declaration that Paul and the audience have become heirs according to the "hope of eternal life" (ἐλπίδα ζωῆς αἰωνίου, 3:7) in the A' unit recalls the apostle's earlier reference to the "hope of eternal life" (ἐλπίδι ζωῆς αἰωνίου, 1:2a) in the A unit. The occurrence of the adjective "eternal" (αἰωνίων) in 1:2c of the A unit strengthens this connection. The identification of believers as "those who have faith in (πεπιστευκότες) God" (3:8a) in the A' unit recalls Paul's self-description as one who "was considered faithful (ἐπιστεύθην) according to the command of God" (1:3) in the A unit. The identification of "Jesus Christ our savior" ('Ἰησοῦ Χριστοῦ τοῦ σωτῆρος ἡμῶν) as the source for the Holy Spirit in 3:6 of the A' unit recalls the identification of "Christ Jesus our savior" (Χριστοῦ 'Ἰησοῦ τοῦ σωτῆρος ἡμῶν) as the source for "grace and peace" in 1:4 of the A unit.

The audience thus experience a development, by way of the chiastically parallel A and A' units, of the central theme of the hope of eternal life in Titus. In the introductory A unit the apostle Paul identifies himself as a "slave of God and apostle of Jesus Christ" (1:1a) "on the basis of the hope of eternal life" (1:2a). Titus, a "true child according to a common faith" (πίστιν)" (1:4), shares in this hope. In the concluding A' unit, Paul identifies believers as "those who have faith in (πεπιστευκότες) God" (3:8a). In addition, Paul's wish of "grace (χάρις) and peace" (1:4), addressed directly to Titus and indirectly to the Cretan community, is addressed now directly to the audience in the final benediction "grace (χάρις) be with all of you" (3:15). In this way, Paul solidifies the relationship between himself, Titus, and the Cretan community. Not only do Titus and the Cretan community share in a "common faith," but they also participate in the "hope of eternal life." In view of this hope—in "recognition of the truth" (1:1b)—the audience are to purse "godliness" according to the exhortation and reproof given by Paul through Titus.

AUDIENCE RESPONSE TO TITUS 1:13B–3:3

*Titus 3:4–8a (A): Saved Not from Works in Righteousness
but for Commendable Works*

In Titus 3:4–8a the audience hear the A element of the fourth and final
chiastic unit (3:4–15) as a mini-chiasm in itself. These verses are composed carefully of three sub-elements:

a. ⁴ But when the kindness (χρηστότης) and the love-for-human-
beings of God (θεοῦ) our savior (σωτῆρος) appeared, ⁵ᵃ not from
works (ἔργων) that we did in righteousness (δικαιοσύνῃ); rather,
according to his mercy,

b. ⁵ᵇ he saved us through the washing of rebirth and renewal of the
Holy Spirit,

a′. ⁶ whom he poured out on us richly through Jesus Christ
(Χριστοῦ) our savior (σωτῆρος), ⁷ so that being made righteous
(δικαιωθέντες) by his grace we might become heirs according to
the hope of eternal life. ⁸ᵃ Faithful is the word, and about these things
I want you to insist, so that those who have faith in God (θεῷ) may be
intent to engage in commendable works (ἔργων).

This mini-chiasm is bracketed by the theme of "works" (ἔργων).
According to the "a" sub-element God demonstrated kindness toward
them "not from works that we did in righteousness; rather, according to
his mercy" (3:5a). Having been saved through the washing of the Holy
Spirit (3:5b), the audience are, according to the "a′" sub-element, to "be
intent to engage in commendable works" (3:8a). God's saving work, then,
both removes confidence in human "works" and inspires a commitment
to "commendable works." The unity of this mini-chiasm is strengthened
by the double reference to God in the parallel sub-elements—"the kindness and the love-for-human-beings of God (θεοῦ) our savior appeared"
in 3:4 and "those who have faith in God (θεῷ)" in 3:8a.

The reference to a distinct divine person—"God our savior" (3:4)[2]
in the "a" sub-element, the "Holy Spirit" (3:5b) in the "b" sub-element,
and "Jesus Christ" (3:6) in the "a′" sub-element—indicates the unity of
each sub-element.[3] The "a" and "a′" sub-elements share multiple linguis-

2. This is likely a reference to God the Father; see 1:3; 2:10b.

3. Spicq (*Les Épîtres Pastorales*, 651–52) comments how 3:4–7 is one of the most
elegant descriptions in the NT on how the various persons of the Trinity work together

tic parallels—"kindness" (χρηστότης) in 3:4 and "Christ" (Χριστοῦ) in 3:6,[4] "God" (θεοῦ) in 3:4 and "God" (θεῷ) in 3:8a, "savior" (σωτῆρος) in 3:4 and 3:6, "works" (ἔργων) in 3:5a and 3:8a, and "righteousness" (δικαιοσύνη) in 3:5a and "made righteous" (δικαιωθέντες) in 3:7. The "b" sub-element contains the main verb "saved" (ἔσωσεν) of the sentence that begins in the "a" sub-element and concludes in the "a'" sub-element.

Titus 3:4–5a (a)

In the closing verse of the third microchiasm (1:13b–3:3) Paul states: "For we too were once (ποτε) ignorant, disobedient, misled, enslaved to various desires and pleasures, spending our lives in evil and envy, despicable, hating one another." The opening words "But when" (ὅτε δέ) of the fourth microchiasm signal a contrast between the audience's former condition (ποτε) and their new situation that has come about through the appearance of "the kindness and love-for-human-beings of God our savior."[5] The verb "appeared" (ἐπεφάνη) recalls for the audience Paul's earlier statement about the "grace of God [that] has appeared (ἐπεφάνη)" (2:14). Here, however, the "grace of God" is specified further in terms of "the kindness and the love-for human-beings of God our savior."[6]

The first noun "kindness" (χρηστότης) occurs frequently in the Psalms as a divine attribute (e.g., Ps 24:7; 30:20; 67:11) and is related to

to accomplish salvation. Witherington (*Letters*, 161 n. 255) adds: "Trinitarian thinking is not just implicit here; it begins to be explicit in texts such as this one. Notice the sort of interlocking or interconnected work as well: the Spirit is poured out through or by means of Jesus."

4. The alliteration between the two terms is demonstrated by the repetition of the first two pairs of consonants χρ and στ.

5. Cf. Hasler, *Die Briefe an Timotheus und Titus*, 96, who argues that 3:4 does not refer to the historical saving-appearance of Christ but merely to revelation in proclamation.

6. As noted earlier—especially in the comments on 2:13—Paul applies the title "savior" (σωτήρ) interchangeably to God the Father (1:3; 2:10a) and Christ Jesus (1:4; 2:13) as a subversive way of indicating Christ's divinity in view of the rhetoric used to characterize Roman emperors who made claims to divinity. The title occurs two more times in 3:4 and 3:6. The phrase "God our savior" (τοῦ σωτῆρος ἡμῶν θεοῦ) in 3:4 is an exact repetition of the phrases found in 1:3 and 2:10a. In 3:6 the term is applied to "Jesus Christ." Thus a clear pattern emerges from these six instances in which the apostle goes back and forth in his references initially to God the Father and then to Christ Jesus as "savior." (For more comments on this pattern, see: Bowman, "Jesus Christ," 749; Knight, *Pastoral Epistles*, 326.) The nouns "kindness" and "love for human beings" in 3:4, therefore, refer to qualities pertaining to God the Father.

the Greek adjective χρηστός, which means "useful" or "serviceable."[7]
Even in the Psalms God's kindness is described in terms of concrete help
(e.g., 84:13). The second noun "love-for-human-beings" (φιλανθρωπία)
occurs in 2 Macc 14:9 as a virtue expected of rulers (see also 2 Macc 9:27;
3 Macc 3:15, 20; 4 Macc 5:12). It also occurs in current Greco-Roman
literature to express general hospitality, idealized descriptions of the gods,
and the imperial cult and its worship (e.g., Claudius *P.Lond.* 1912.102;
Dio Cassius *Rom. Hist.* 73.5.2; Philo *Legat* 67).[8]

The combination of the two nouns "kindness and love-for-human-
beings" is familiar to the audience, possibly even a cliché used of benefactors and emperors.[9] God, then, is presented not only as a benefactor
but also as the true emperor who shows "kindness and love-for-human-
beings." The proximity of this description to the exhortation to "submit
to ruling authorities" (3:1) conveys to the audience that while they must
obey "ruling authorities," they are to reject any imperial claims to divinity.
The rhetoric of "kindness and love-for-human-beings" is appropriate only
with respect to God in Christ Jesus. This association is suggested by the
assonances between "kindness" (χρηστότης) and "Christ" (Χριστός).
Despite previous uses of the phrase the audience are to understand and
apply it now uniquely to God in Christ.

Verse 4 comes as a tremendous challenge to the audience. As their
"savior" God deserves their full allegiance; that is, they are to re-pattern
their lives after the one who has saved them from their ignorance, enslavement, and hostility (3:2). The audience take special notice of the noun
φιλανθρωπία because it echoes the command to show "all gentleness
to all human beings (ἀνθρώπους)" (3:1) and reminds them of how the
"grace of God" is "bringing salvation to all human beings (ἀνθρώποις)"
(2:11). That "God our savior" has demonstrated such "love-for-human-
beings" (φιλανθρωπία) in Jesus Christ provides the basis and power for
the audience's own "love-for-human-beings";[10] thus the elder should be a
"lover-of-strangers" (φιλόξενον) and "lover-of-goodness" (φιλάγαθον,
1:8); and the "younger women" "lovers-of-husbands" (φιλάνδρους) and
"lovers-of-children" (φιλοτέκνους, 2:4).[11]

---

7. LSJ, s.v.

8. See Towner, *Letters*, 778.

9. Witherington, *Letters*, 156.

10. See Johnson, *Letters*, 248.

11. Towner observes the subversive implications of 3:4: "People are to exhibit these

The apostle begins 3:5a abruptly with the phrase "not from works that we did in righteousness" to highlight the gracious basis of God's salvation. The phrase "works that we did in righteousness" refers to "works" (ἔργων) done "in" (ἐν) the sphere or state of "righteousness" (δικαιοσύνῃ), i.e., "works" done while living "sensibly and righteously (δικαίως) and godly in the present age" (2:12). This new state is the result of the "work" of Christ Jesus "who gave himself on behalf of us, so that he might redeem us from all lawlessness and cleanse for himself a special people, zealous for commendable works (ἔργων)" (2:14). The verb "did" (ἐποιήσαμεν) is almost superfluous but is included to set up a contrast between the actions "we did" and what God did in Christ.

The apostle reiterates the unmerited quality of God's kindness point by completing the contrast at the end of the "a" sub-element: "rather, according to his mercy." The adversative ἀλλά occurred several times already in the letter to express a strong contrast. It is not enough for the elder to lack vices; "rather" (ἀλλά) he must also demonstrate virtues (1:7-8). While "all things are clean to the clean," "to the defiled and unfaithful nothing is clean; rather (ἀλλά), defiled are both their mind and conscience" (1:15). Christian "slaves" are not to be "those who pilfer; rather (ἀλλά) those who demonstrate that all faith is good" (2:10a). The same force of the adversative is operative here. The preposition "according to" (κατά) and the pronoun "his" (αὐτοῦ) further the contrast: it is "not *from* works that *we* did in righteousness" but "*according to his* mercy." The noun "mercy" (ἔλεος)—which is a synonym for "grace" (1:4)—further highlights the unmerited quality of God's "kindness." "Recognition of the truth" (1:1b) demands recognizing that the gift of "eternal life" is solely "according to his mercy"—completely independent of human works, as Paul alluded to already in the clause, "God, who cannot lie, promised [eternal life] *before eternal times*" (1:2b-c). While Paul highlights that the redeemed are to be "zealous for commendable works" (2:14) and "ready for all good work" (3:1) in contrast to the opponents who are "unqualified for all good work" (1:16), he does not want the audience to suppose even for a moment that their works earn God's favor.

---

qualities of God in their own lives, and in framing the life of faith in this way a somewhat subversive intention may again be detected: qualities that Greco-Roman culture ascribes to the ideal 'ruler' are actually to be exhibited by ordinary Christians in society. The advent of Christ turns assumptions and values on their heads" (*Letters*, 779).

Titus 3:5b (b)

Having established the basis of salvation, in 3:5b Paul states its means (διά): "he saved us through the washing of rebirth and renewal of the Holy Spirit." The clause "he saved us" (ἔσωσεν ἡμᾶς) is somewhat redundant given that in 3:4 he refers to God as "our savior" (σωτῆρος ἡμῶν). The redundancy, however, reiterates the centrality of the theme of salvation in the letter. Moreover, the aorist tense communicates to the audience that God is not only capable of saving (God is a savior), but also that he has already carried out the work of salvation (God has saved).

The prepositional phrase that follows is dense with meaning, but the grammatical interrelation between the genitive nouns that follow is unclear.[12] The literal translation "through the washing of rebirth and renewal of the Holy Spirit" yields many variations, but two main proposals for arranging the nouns have been suggested.[13] First, salvation is effected through two distinct operations—"through the washing of rebirth and (through) the renewal of the Holy Spirit." Second the "washing" by the Spirit results in the single complex of "rebirth and renewal"—"through the washing of (i.e., that effects) rebirth and renewal." Two factors support to the second arrangement. First, the terms "rebirth" (παλιγγενεσίας) and "renewal" (ἀνακαινώσεως) are nearly synonymous, suggesting a single complex; the conjunction "and" (καί), then, is epexegetical.[14] Second, both terms are governed by the single preposition "through" (διά).[15] Hence, a single effect is in view presented from two different but interrelated perspectives.[16]

The previous references to "clean" (1:15) describe an inner spiritual condition that involves redemption from "lawlessness" and transformative cleansing (2:14). The "washing" (λουτροῦ) in view, therefore, refers to spiritual cleansing,[17] not physical baptism.[18] This position is strengthened by the syntactical link between "washing" and the "Holy Spirit"

---

12. See Marshall, *Pastoral Epistles*, 316–22.

13. See Towner, *Letters*, 783.

14. See Spicq, *Les Épîtres Pastorales*, 653; Towner, *Goal of Our Instruction*, 115.

15. See Dunn, *Baptism in the Holy Spirit*, 155–56; Fee, *God's Empowering Presence*, 781.

16. See Quinn, *Letter*, 218–19.

17. See Mounce, *Pastoral Epistles*, 448–49.

18. Cf. Kelly, *Pastoral Epistles*, 252.

(πνεύματος ἁγίου); thus spiritual cleansing is accomplished by the Spirit.[19] Verse 5b both encourages and empowers the audience. According to 3:3 they were "enslaved to various desires and pleasures," a condition that is implied by the redemptive language of 2:14. But now, as a result of "the kindness and the love-for-human-beings of God" (3:4), they have experienced "rebirth and renewal"; consequently, they are now empowered "for all good work" (3:1).

Titus 3:6–8a (a')

Continuing his discussion on "the kindness and the love-for-human-beings of God" (3:4), Paul adds in 3:6, "whom he poured out on us richly through Jesus Christ our savior." Both the verb and adverb highlight God's generosity. The verb "poured out" (ἐξέχεεν) depicts liquid being pouring out, resulting in a "full experience."[20] The adverb "richly" (πλουσίως) expresses similarly "in full measure."[21] The audience perceive that God has not withheld his "Spirit," but has given it "richly" such that they are now enabled "for all good work" (1:16): because they have been redeemed "from all lawlessness" (2:14) by God who has given his "all," they are now able to show "all gentleness to all human beings" (3:2) in a supernatural manner.

The clause bears strong resemblance to Joel 3:1:

Titus 3:6: οὗ ἐξέχεεν ἐφ' ἡμᾶς πλουσίως

Joel 3:1: καὶ ἐκχεῶ ἀπὸ τοῦ πνεύματός μου ἐπὶ πᾶσαν σάρκα

According to 1:2a-3 an important shift has taken place in salvation history: eternal life, which was "promised before eternal times," has now been "revealed" through the apostle's "proclamation." Paul's declaration that the "Holy Spirit" has now been "poured out" reiterates this progress in salvation history. Therefore, the audience must recognize that they no longer live in the "former" age of the flesh, "spending our lives in evil and envy" (3:3), but in the eschatological age of the Spirit. Recognizing their unique place in redemptive history is a central concern for the apostle.

The phrase "Jesus Christ our savior" is the third instance when the phrase "God our savior" (3:4) is followed immediately by the phrase "Jesus

19. Note again strong echoes of Ezek 36:25–27.
20. BDAG, s.v.
21. UBS lexicon.

Christ our savior" (see 1:3, 4; 2:10, 13). That God the Father "poured out" the Spirit "through Jesus Christ our savior (διὰ Ἰησοῦ Χριστοῦ τοῦ σωτῆρος ἡμῶν)" recalls for the audience the apostle's earlier prayer wish of "grace and peace from God the Father and Christ Jesus our savior (Χριστοῦ Ἰησοῦ τοῦ σωτῆρος ἡμῶν)" (1:4). In both instances the source of blessing is both "God the Father" who is "our savior (σωτῆρος)" and "Christ Jesus" who is also "our savior (σωτῆρος)." The divinity of Christ, therefore, is implied again.

At the same time the pouring out of the "Holy Spirit," which is so extensive that it results in a "full experience," raises the question of how the immaterial is experienced by the material. The phrase "Jesus Christ our savior" recalls for the audience the "grace of God [that] has appeared" (2:11)—when the divine became human—and thus answers this question: through the appearance of the God-man in "Jesus Christ" Paul and the audience have received the full outpouring of the Spirit. God's "kindness" (χρηστότης, 3:4) in pouring out the "Holy Spirit" is given through "Christ" (Χριστοῦ). The prepositional phrase "through Jesus Christ our savior," therefore, deepens the audience's appreciation of the first appearance of the "grace of God": through this event they have received the Spirit who transforms and empowers them to "live sensibly and righteously and godly in the present age" (2:12). Moreover, the audience now perceive that the "grace and peace from God the Father and Christ Jesus our savior" are now theirs through the outpouring of the Spirit, the gift of God the Father given through Jesus Christ.

Concluding the extended sentence that began in 3:4, Paul states in 3:7: "so that being made righteous by his grace we might become heirs according to the hope of eternal life." The passive voice of the participle "made righteous" (δικαιωθέντες) reiterates that "God our savior," who "saved us" (3:5b) and "poured out on us richly" (3:6) his Spirit, is still the main subject of the entire sentence. The participle echoes its cognate noun "righteousness" (δικαιοσύνη, 3:5) and adverb "righteously" (δικαίως, 2:14). Paul's point to the audience is that believers have been "made righteous," i.e., transferred into the sphere of "righteousness" by the initiative and power of God. Consequently they are now able to live "righteously."

The phrase "by his grace (χάριτι)" recalls for the audience the blessing of further "grace" (χάρις, 1:4), which is the gracious love and empowering presence of God. In addition, the audience are reminded of the "grace (χάρις) of God [that] has appeared, saving all human beings" (2:11), i.e., the climactic expression of God's love and power. Now the audience are told that it is "by his grace" they have been "made righteous." Thus they now understand that the very "grace" that made them righteous is the same "grace" that will empower them to live righteously in the present age.

The conjunction "so that" (ἵνα) communicates to the audience God's purpose in salvation—that "we might become heirs according to the hope of eternal life." The noun "heirs" (κληρονόμοι) refers to people who have become beneficiaries.[22] According to this mini-chiasm, all believers have become beneficiaries of "the kindness and the love-for-human-beings of God our savior" (3:4). Specifically, they have received "richly" the gift of the "Holy Spirit" (3:5b–6). The LXX correlations between election and inheritance (e.g., Exod 15:17; Josh 1:15; Ps 32:12) remind the audience of their own election (1:1a) and calling to be a "special people, zealous for commendable works" (2:14).

The apostle, however, does not specify what their inheritance is in the closing prepositional phrase of 3:7; nor does he suggest that the "elect of God" (1:1a) have "become heirs in hope of eternal life" (*NAB*)—i.e., "with the confident expectation of eternal life" (*NET*), although this is true. Rather, he states that the "elect" have "become heirs according to the hope of eternal life (κατ' ἐλπίδα ζωῆς αἰωνίου)." The preposition "according to" communicates to the audience that they have "become heirs according to" the plan of salvation that is outlined in 1:2a-3. "According to" this plan God promised "eternal life" (ζωῆς αἰωνίου, 1:2a) "before eternal times" (πρὸ χρόνων αἰωνίων, 1:2c) and has "revealed" it now through the apostle's "proclamation" (1:3). Thus Paul seeks to express again the redemptive framework "according to" which the audience are "to be ready for all good work." Recognizing that they have "become heirs according to the hope of eternal life"—"according to" this grand scheme of redemption, the audience understand that the proper response is to "live sensibly and righteously and godly in the present age" and to be "zealous for commendable works" (2:14). The "hope of eternal life," then, not only provides the motivation for living as a "slave of God and apostle of Jesus Christ" (1:2a), but also a specific framework—bracketed by the first and second appearance of God's grace—for righteous living.

22. BDAG, s.v.

In the first half of 3:8a Paul states: "Faithful is the word, and about these things I want you to insist."[23] The juxtaposition of the "word" (λόγος) and "hope of eternal life" (3:7) recalls for the audience the anacoluthon of the opening verses to the letter where Paul shifts the object from "eternal life that God, who cannot lie, promised" to the "word" (λόγον) that he "revealed at the proper time" (1:2a-3). "Word" in 3:8a, then, is a reference to the "word of God" (2:5) concerning "eternal life" that was "revealed . . . in the proclamation" and entrusted first to the apostle (1:3) and now to Titus (2:8) and the elders (1:9b).[24] Echoing the earlier phrase "faithful word" (πιστοῦ λόγου, 1:9a), Paul declares that the "word" is "faithful" (πιστός); that is, it is believable because it comes from "God, who cannot lie" (1:2b). Thus it stands in contrast to "word" of the "unfaithful" (ἀπίστοις, 1:15) who are "teaching what is not necessary" (1:11) and "who turn away from the truth" (1:14).

The apostle, however, is not merely echoing his earlier statement that the "word" is "faithful." This mini-chiasm describes salvation in terms of "rebirth and renewal" (3:5): having received the Spirit and "being made righteous" (3:6-7), the audience are no longer "enslaved to various desires and pleasures" (3:3) but transferred into the sphere of "righteousness" (3:5). The adjective "faithful" (πιστός), therefore, carries a dynamic sense, communicating to the audience that the "word" is also "faithful" because it elicits and strengthens true "faith." This dynamic and transformative aspect of the "word" is suggested earlier in 1:1a, 1:13, and 2:1–10a. Paul's "proclamation" of the "word" is "according to the faith (πίστιν) of the elect of God" (1:1a). Thus the audience's "faith" is strengthened by listening carefully to the letter. By "holding fast to the faithful word (πιστ̂ ̓ τοῦ λόγου)" Titus, the model elder, must "reprove severely, so that [those who oppose] might be sound in the faith (πίστει)" (1:13). Similarly, by speaking "what is consistent with sound doctrine" (2:1) Titus strengthens the "faith" (2:2, 10a) of the various members of God's household. This dynamic power of the "faithful word" is now made explicit in 3:8a. Recognizing this dimension of the "word," the audience understand better why the elder must be an individual who "holds fast to the faithful

---

23. For a detailed study of the "faithful sayings" in the Pastoral Epistles, see Knight, *The Faithful Sayings in the Pastoral Letters*.

24. Some argue that the "word" refers to what follows in the text; see, e.g., Campbell, "Identifying the Faithful Sayings in the Pastoral Epistles," 73–86. This position is unpersuasive.

word" (1:9a) and why they themselves must stop "paying attention to Jewish myths and regulations of human beings who turn away from the truth" (1:14). By listening to the "faithful word" that is communicated presently through the letter to Titus and reiterated through the person of Titus, the audience's "faith" is strengthened.

What "these things" (τούτων) refers to is debated,[25] but the shift from the singular "word" to the plural "these things" and the conjunction kai, between the noun "word" and the preposition "about" suggest that Paul has in mind more than just doctrinal instruction. Through exhortation and reproof Titus is also to "insist" on the lifestyle that accords with "recognition of the truth," specifically the reminders given in 3:1–2. The statement "I want you to insist" carries the same tone as the command, "Let no one disregard you" (2:15b). When the verb "want" (βούλομαι) is used with an accusative (σε) and an infinitive (διαβεβαιοῦσθαι), it expresses a strong command.[26] The verb "insist" means to "speak confidently."[27] Aware of the presence and influence of the "rebels, empty-talkers and deceivers," the apostle expresses to Titus that even if a person were to "disregard you (σου)" (2:15b), "I want you to insist" on "truth" and "godliness" (1:1a). Titus, therefore, is reminded again that he is in Crete according to the apostle's directive (1:5). The audience are also reminded of Titus's representative authority and the need to submit to him in recognition of Paul's own authority as an "apostle of Jesus Christ" (1:1a).

The mini-chiasm concludes with the purpose (ἵνα) statement "so that those who have faith in God may be intent to engage in good works." The participial phrase "those who have faith in God" (οἱ πεπιστευκότες θεῷ) refers to those who believe that the "word" is "faithful" (πιστός); to "those who have faith" in the proclamation of which the apostle the apostle "was considered faithful" (ἐπιστεύθην) according to the command of God (θεοῦ) our savior" (1:3); to those who hold fast to "the faithful (πιστοῦ) word that is according to the teaching" (1:9a), i.e., to those who believe in the first and second appearance of Christ and who believe that God's salvation is not according to works but mercy.

The phrase "commendable works" (καλῶν ἔργων) reminds the audience not only of Titus's specific calling to be a "model of commendable

---

25. See the different proposals in Johnson, *Letters*, 250; Quinn, *Letter*, 241; Towner, *Letters*, 791 n. 81.

26. See Marshall, *Pastoral Epistles*, 330.

27. BDAG, s.v.

works (καλῶν ἔργων)" (2:7) but also of their general calling to be a "special people, zealous for commendable works (καλῶν ἔργων)" (2:14). "Commendable works," which should be characteristic both of their conduct towards other believers and towards the watching world, are part and parcel of their new existence. Formerly they were under the power of "lawlessness"; now through Christ they have been redeemed and cleansed (2:14). Formerly, they were "ignorant, disobedient, misled, enslaved to various desires and pleasures, spending [their] lives in evil and envy, despicable, hating one another" (3:3); now they have been "made righteous by his grace" (3:7). Consequently, they are to pursue their identity as a "special people, zealous for commendable works" (2:14); they are to "be intent to engage in commendable works" (φροντίζωσιν καλῶν ἔργων προΐστασθαι). The wordy and somewhat redundant combination "[to] be intent to engage" highlights Paul's concern for conduct that accords with "recognition of the truth" (1:1a).

Titus 3:8b-9a (B): Focusing on Commendable Things

The demonstrative "these" (ταῦτα) refers both to the "word" (3:8a) and the related exhortations and reproofs concerning "godliness."[28] Titus is to insist "about these things" (τούτων) because "these things" are "commendable" (καλά)—they give rise to "commendable (καλῶν) works" (3:8a) and are "useful" (ὠφέλιμα) to "human beings." Thus Paul highlights that it is not just "commendable works" that are "useful" to "human beings" but also the doctrine, exhortation, and reproof behind them. The noun "human beings" (ἀνθρώποις) recalls for the audience the command to show "all gentleness to all human beings (ἀνθρώπους)" (3:2). The reference is to the outside watching world among whom the audience are to demonstrate the respectability and benefit of their profession of faith and zeal "for commendable works" (2:14). In this way, they serve "in the present age" (2:12) as the means through which the "grace of God" saves "all human beings (ἀνθρώποις)" (2:11).

In 3:9a Paul commands Titus and the Cretan community to "avoid foolish inquiries and genealogies and rivalries and quarrels about the law." The contrast between what they are to "be intent to engage in" (3:8a) and what they are to "avoid" is indicated by the disjunction "but" (δέ).

---

28. There is some disagreement over the antecedent. See, e.g., Barrett *Pastoral Epistles*, 144–45; Fee, *Titus*, 207–8; Mounce, *Pastoral Epistles*, 453.

That these activities function in a complementary manner is suggested by the verb itself: Titus is commanded to "avoid" (περιΐστασο) certain things while insisting "about these things" (περὶ τούτων, 3:8a). "Foolish inquiries and genealogies and rivalries and quarrels about the law," then, stand in clear contrast to "these things"—the "word" (3:8a) and its corollary exhortations and reproofs. This complementary style of exhortation reminds the audience of Paul's earlier comments that "soundness" comes from "holding fast (ἀντεχόμενον) to the faithful word" (1:9a) and "not paying attention (προσέχοντες) to Jewish myths and regulations of human beings" (1:14).

The list of what things are to be avoided recalls for the audience Paul's earlier description of the opposition in 1:10–13a and 1:13b–16.[29] The audience recognize, therefore, that the presence and influence of the false teachers continues to loom in the apostle's mind. Paul mentions four interrelated items. The word "inquiries" (ζητήσεις) is the abstract of the verb ζητέω, which means "to look for" or "to examine."[30] The noun occurs regularly in Greco-Roman literature to describe philosophical "inquiries" (e.g., Plato PLT 262c). The adjective "foolish" (μωράς) refers generally to someone or something that is "stupid," but in the LXX suggests occasionally spiritual ignorance (e.g., Deut 32:6; Isa 32:6; Jer 5:21). The "inquiries" in view are "foolish" because they are done by "human beings who turn away from the truth" (1:14) and who have demonstrated that they are "vile and disobedient and unqualified for all good work" (1:16).

The precise reference for "genealogies" (γενεαλογίας) is debated.[31] Various works from Greco-Roman literature link "genealogies" with myths (e.g., Plato Tim 22a). Therefore, "genealogies" is likely a reference to "Jewish myths" and details further for the audience the content of what is being taught by "human beings who turn away from the truth" (1:14). It may also be a subtle reference to the Cretan tendency to identify themselves as the guardians of the birthplace and tomb of Zeus.[32] Having experienced the "washing of rebirth and renewal of the Holy Spirit" (3:5), the audience have a new genealogy in Christ Jesus that began through the

29. See Fee, Titus, 210, who suggests a chiastic relation between 1:10–16 and 3:9–11.

30. BDAG, s.v.

31. See Marshall, Pastoral Epistles, 335–36, for various proposals.

32. See Wieland, "Roman Crete," 345.

appearance of the "grace of God" (2:11). Thus they are to establish their identity on the basis of the person and work of Christ.

The noun "rivalries" (ἔρεις) refers specifically to "engagement in rivalry, especially with reference to positions taken in a matter."[33] "Rivalries" reminds the audience of the divisive nature of the "rebels, empty-talkers and deceivers" (1:10) "who are upsetting whole households, teaching what is not necessary" (1:11). Being "human beings who turn away from the truth" (1:14), they stand as rivals to Paul, who is a "slave of God and apostle of Jesus Christ according to the faith of the elect of God and recognition of the truth" (1:1a–b).

Finally, Titus and the Cretan community are to "avoid . . . quarrels about the law." Given Paul's earlier mention of "circumcision" (1:10) and "Jewish myths" (1:14), the adjective "law" (νομικάς) refers to Jewish law, especially on matters of purity and defilement (1:15). As noted earlier, the noun "quarrels" (μάχας) refers to "battles fought without actual weapons";[34] hence, an emphasis on words. The noun reminds the audience of the exhortation "to be unquarrelsome" (ἀμάχους, 3:2). The earlier exhortation expresses a general command "to be unquarrelsome, kind, demonstrating all gentleness to all human beings" (3:2). The phrase "quarrels about the law" is not only a specific application of this general command but also a signal to the audience that the apostle is shifting his focus from outside "human beings" to internal matters pertaining to God's "special people" (2:14). These things are to be "avoided" because they are "useless and worthless" and "do not reflect the character of the Savior, who is kind and loving and builds up others."[35]

Titus 3:9b–13 (B')

The B' element begins by explaining briefly why Titus and the Cretan community are to "avoid foolish controversies and genealogies and rivalries and quarrels about the law": "for they are useless and empty" (3:9b). The two adjectives communicate to the audience two important points. The first adjective "useless" (ἀνωφελεῖς) establishes a clear contrast with 3:8b where Paul states, "These are commendable and useful (ὠφέλιμα) to human beings." The second adjective "empty" (μάταιοι) reminds the

33. BDAG, s.v.
34. See comments on 3:2.
35. Witherington, *Letters*, 162.

audience of Paul's first explicit description of the opponents as "rebels, empty-talkers (ματαιολόγοι) and deceivers" (1:10). The apostle's intention, then, is not simply to censure these "foolish controversies and genealogies and rivalries and quarrels about the law" as "empty" but—more importantly—to associate them with the "empty-talkers." In turn the audience's assessment of the opponents' "teaching" descends even further from "not necessary" (1:11) to "foolish" (3:9a) and "useless and empty" (3:9b).

In 3:10–11 the apostle provides further instruction on how to deal with a "heretical human being." The instructions presuppose the possibility and hope of restoration. The adjective "heretical" (αἱρετικόν) applies to a "human being" (ἄνθρωπον) who is "factious, division-making."[36] It is an apt description of the "rebels, empty-talkers and deceivers" who are "upsetting whole households, teaching what is not necessary" (1:10–11). Such "human beings (ἀνθρώπων) who turn away from the truth" (1:14) cause divisions inevitably among the audience. "After a first and second (μετὰ μίαν καὶ δευτέραν) warning" Titus and the Cretan community are to "dismiss" this sort of individual. "Warning" (νουθεσίαν) refers specifically to "counsel about avoidance or cessation of an improper course of conduct."[37] Here the "improper course of conduct" includes "teaching what is not necessary for this reason—shameful gain" (1:11); propagating "Jewish myths and regulations of human beings" (1:14); and devoting oneself to "foolish controversies and genealogies and rivalries and quarrels about the law" (3:9a) instead of "holding fast to the faithful word that is according to the teaching" (1:9a).

"After a first and second warning," the audience are to "dismiss" (παραιτοῦ) the individual—to view him as someone who is not "according to a common faith" (1:4)—to "remove [him] from the fellowship of the Christian community."[38] The reminder to show "all gentleness to all human beings (ἀνθρώπους)" (3:2) indicates that the dismissal of this sort of "human being" is different from mistreatment. At the same time, the audience are not to look to such a "heretical human being" as a guide for "truth" and "godliness" (1:1b).

36. BDAG, s.v.

37. BDAG, s.v.

38. Knight, *Pastoral Epistles*, 355.

The audience are to "dismiss a heretical human being, knowing that such a person is perverted and sinning, being self-decided" (3:11). The participle "knowing" (εἰδώς) echoes the confident claims of the opposition who "profess to know (εἰδέναι)" God (1:16). The apostle wants the audience to have such confidence, "knowing" several things. First, the perfect participle "perverted" (ἐξέστραπται) describes a person that has turned from "what is considered true or morally proper."[39] The participle bears some similarity to the participles "upsetting" (ἀνατρέπουσιν, 1:11) and "who turn away from" (ἀποστρεφομένων, 1:14). Paul's subtle message is that "perverted" ones "who turn away from the truth" are responsible for "upsetting whole households, teaching what is not necessary." "Such a person" (ὁ τοιοῦτος) is the antitype of the elder who is "holding fast to the faithful word that is according to the teaching" (1:9a).[40] Second, by disregarding the repeated warnings, "such a person" is "sinning" (ἁμαρτάνει). "Sinning" indicates a willful and informed mistake against God. Thus the sense of 3:10–11 is: "Dismiss a heretical human being, knowing that such a person is perverted and sinning" knowingly. The present tense of the verb highlights how "such a person" is "sinning" even now not only by continually "teaching what is not necessary" (1:11) but also by ignoring the multiple attempts to be reconciled into the community of faith; his "sinning" is completely deliberate. In this respect the final remark "being self-decided" (ὢν αὐτοκατάκριτος) is self-explanatory. Being without the excuse of ignorance "after a first and second warning" and living knowingly and willfully in sin, "such a person" must be dismissed by the audience.

In Titus 3:12a-13 the audience hear the B' element of the final chiastic unit (3:4–15) as a mini-chiasm in itself. These verses are composed carefully of three sub-elements:

a. [12a] When I send (πέμψω) Artemas to you or Tychicus, hasten (σπούδασον) to come to me at Nicopolis,

b. [12b] for I have decided to winter there.

a'. [13] Zenas the lawyer and Apollos hastily send (σπουδαίως πρόπεμψον), so that nothing is lacking for them.

39. BDAG, s.v.

40. Towner (*Letters*, 798 n. 19) suggests a "pejorative categorizing use of this demonstrative [τοιοῦτος]"; see also Marshall, *Pastoral Epistles*, 339 n. 129.

This mini-chiasm is bracketed by two personal commands. In addition, the "a" and "a'" sub-elements are bidirectional with the apostle sending Artemas or Tychicus to Titus, and Titus and the Cretan community sending Zenas and Apollos to Paul. The repetition of the related terms—all of which occur uniquely in this mini-chiasm—"send" (πέμψω) and "hasten" (σπούδασον) in 3:12a and "send" (πρόπεμψον) and "hastily" (σπουδαίως) in 3:13 evidences the deliberate parallelism in view.

Titus 3:12a (a)

In 3:12a Paul says, "When I send Artemas to you or Tychicus, hasten to come to me at Nicopolis." From this personal note the audience learn two things. First, the verb "send" has an official ring, denoting "dispatch."[41] Thus the audience are introduced to the individual who will serve in Crete as Paul's new "true child according to a common faith" (1:4).[42] In turn they are to show this person the same respect and submission that Titus merits. The audience are also reminded of the apostle's constant concern for them to provide faithful leaders. Second, the audience's suspicion from the language of 1:5 that Titus's tenure with them is provisional is confirmed by the temporal conjunction "when" (ὅταν) and the command "hasten to come to me." The conjunction indicates a condition that will be fulfilled in the near future. The command "hasten" (σπούδασον) conveys both a sense of determination and speed: Titus must make every effort "to come to me at Nicopolis" as quickly as possible.[43] The verb suggests also that Titus is as much needed at Nicopolis as he is in Crete. In this way Paul reiterates subtly to the audience his high esteem for Titus. Realizing that Titus's departure is imminent, the audience appreciate more deeply the urgency of establishing elders and dismissing false teachers.

Titus 3:12b (b)

The pivot of the mini-chiasm states simply Paul's decision to "winter there" (1:12b). The verb "have decided" (κέκρικα) indicates a firm decision akin to a "heretical human being's" decision to disregard a "first and second warning" and who is therefore "self-decided" (αὐτοκατάκριτος,

---

41. BDAG, s.v.

42. "Artemas" is not mentioned anywhere else in the NT. For "Tychicus" (assuming he is the same person who traveled with Paul) see Acts 20:4; Eph 6:21; Col 4:7; 2 Tim 4:12.

43. For more information on "Nicopolis," see Collins, *Titus*, 372.

3:11). In this sense, it reiterates that the heretic's decision to remain sin is intentional and exhibits a sense of determination. The decision "to winter" (παραχειμάσαι) in Nicopolis likely surprises the Cretan community, given Nicopolis is notorious for its harsh winters.[44] Apparently the city is an ideal location for further ministry.[45] The apostle's resolve, then, to "winter there" reiterates for the audience Paul's commitment to fulfill his apostolic calling. In contrast to the opponents who are "teaching what is not necessary for this reason—shameful gain" (1:11) Paul ministers in harsh environments "on the basis of the hope of eternal life" (1:2a).

Titus 3:13 (a')

In the "a'" sublement Paul adds one more personal instruction: "Zenas the lawyer and Apollos hastily send."[46] It is noteworthy that Paul states Zenas's profession but does not do so for Apollos. This inclusion indicates Paul's effort to reinforce the linguistic connection between the B element where the audience are told to "avoid . . . quarrels about the law (νομικάς)" (3:9a) and the B' element where Zenas is described as "the lawyer" (νομικόν, 3:13).[47] The title "lawyer" indicates that he is "learned in the law, an expert in Mosaic or non-Mosaic law."[48] His Greek name suggests the latter, namely, Greek or Roman law, but the chiastic progression from the B element makes it likely that the Mosaic Law is in view. Using terms similar to "send" (πέμψω) and "hasten" (σπούδασον) in 3:12a, Paul commands the audience to "send hastily" (σπουδαίως πρόπεμψον) these two individuals. The use of πρόπεμψον communicates to the audience that they are not only to send these individuals, but also to aid them in their journey by providing basic needs and money.[49]

The purpose (ἵνα) behind the command "send hastily" is "so that nothing is lacking for them." The verb "is lacking" (λείπῃ) recalls for the audience Paul's earlier statement: "For this reason I left (ἀπέλιπον) you

44. See Towner, *Letters*, 801.

45. See Witherington, *Letters*, 165.

46. "Zenas" is not mentioned anywhere else in the NT. For "Apollos" (assuming he is the same person associated with Paul in the Corinth-Ephesus mission) see Acts 18:24; 19:1; 1 Cor 1:12; 3:4, 5, 6, 22; 4:6; 16:12.

47. Cf. Towner, *Letters*, 801: "Speculation as to why the description 'the lawyer' is included with his name remains largely just that—speculation."

48. BDAG, s.v.

49. BDAG, s.v.

in Crete, so that what is left (τὰ λείποντα) you might set right" (1:5). In contrast to the churches in Crete, which are "lacking" elders, Zenas and Apollos are to lack "nothing" (μηδέν). The audience's calling "to be ready for all good work" (3:1) includes the "good work" of meeting the practical needs of those who minister among them.

Titus 3:14–15 (A')

The apostle's concern for Zenas and Apollos—"that nothing is lacking for them"—provides an opportunity to reiterate the command to "engage in commendable works"; hence he begins the A' element of the fourth chiasm (3:4–15) with the exhortation: "And let also our own learn to engage in commendable works." The force of δὲ καί is disputed,[50] but the pronoun "our own" (ἡμέτεροι) focuses on the Cretan community; thus the sense is, "'our own' (the Cretan community)—alongside you personally (Titus)" must do the "good work" (3:1) of ensuring that "nothing is lacking for them." The use of the pronoun "our own" at this juncture is also important because it recalls for the audience the repeated occurrences of the pronoun "our" (1:3, 4; 2:8, 10, 12, 13, 14; 3:3, 4, 5, 6, 12), especially in association with "God our (ἡμῶν) savior" and "Christ Jesus our (ἡμῶν) savior." The pronoun ἡμέτεροι reiterates for the audience both their bond with Paul and Titus and their separation from "human beings who turn away from the truth" (1:14).

The verb "to learn" (μανθανέτωσαν) carries the sense of learning mainly through experience.[51] In this instance the "experience" is that of providing sufficiently for Zenas and Apollos. The phrase "to engage in commendable works" (καλῶν ἔργων προΐστασθαι) is an obvious repetition of the phrase in 3:8a. Paul's intention is to specify and materialize the general command given earlier by including the phrase "urgent needs."[52] The adjective "urgent" (ἀναγκαίας) stresses the pressing and indispensable nature of these "needs."[53] The term "needs" (χρείας) pertains to livelihood—food, water, shelter, and clothing.[54] The phrase

---

50. For various proposals, see Marshall, *Pastoral Epistles*, 345 n. 17.

51. BDAG, s.v. See also Quinn, *Letter*, 267–68.

52. The combination was apparently a stock phrase; see the multiple examples in Spicq, *Les Épîtres Pastorales*, 693.

53. BDAG, s.v.

54. BDAG, s.v.

"urgent needs" is somewhat redundant, possibly focusing the audience on "needs" that are especially urgent. Here, for instance, the suggestion is that Zenas and Apollos must leave soon but cannot until their "urgent needs" are met. The audience realize, therefore, that "to be intent to engage in commendable works" (3:8a) means "to be intent" on meeting the "urgent needs" of people in general but especially church leaders like Zenas and Apollos. In contrast to the opponents who engage in abstract "controversies and genealogies and rivalries and quarrels about the law" (3:9a), the audience are to "learn to engage in commendable works" that meet people's basic and concrete needs by actually doing so.

The purpose clause, "so that they might not be unfruitful," is stated negatively to draw a deliberate contrast with the "unfruitful" (ἄκαρποι) troublemakers who are "unqualified all every good work" (1:16). Instead of building up the churches they are "upsetting whole households, teaching what is not necessary" (1:11). Instead of "holding fast to the faithful word" (1:9a) they are focusing the "elect" (1:1a) on "Jewish myths and regulations of human beings" (1:14). Instead of "demonstrating all gentleness to all human beings" (3:2) they are causing the "word of God" (2:5) to be blasphemed. That "our own" "might not (mh,) be unfruitful" is not simply a general description of the "elect of God" (1:1a) but a deliberate contrast with the "rebels, empty-talkers and deceivers" (1:10). Thus this purpose clause implicitly exhorts the audience to be fruitful and reproves the opponents for being "unfruitful."

Verse 14 summarizes the concern and content of the letter to Titus. The phrase "commendable works" reminds the audience of the appearance of the "grace of God" (2:11) in "Jesus Christ, who gave himself on behalf of us, so that he might redeem us from all lawlessness and cleanse for himself a special people, zealous for commendable works" (2:14). "Through the washing of rebirth and renewal of the Holy Spirit" (3:5) Paul, Titus, and the Cretan community have "become heirs according to the hope of eternal life" (3:7). "Recognition of the truth" must accord with "godliness" (1:1b)—a commitment "to engage in commendable works." Exhortation and reproof according "to the faithful word that is according to the teaching" (1:9a) from Paul, Titus, and the future elders, and the response of practical obedience from the audience will produce lives that are not "unfruitful."

Paul concludes the letter and the fourth microchiasm with a series of greetings and a final blessing. First, Paul conveys greetings on behalf of "all who are with me" (οἱ μετ᾽ ἐμοῦ πάντες). Paul does not specify the identity of this group but rather describes them generally as those who are "with (μετά) me" possibly because Titus and the Cretan community do not know those traveling with Paul. But it may also be a subtle way of expressing a sense of camaraderie between those who are of a "common faith" (1:4) in distinction to those "who turn away from the truth" (1:14).

Second, Paul commands Titus to "greet those who love us in the faith (πίστει)." In the introduction to the letter, Paul described Titus as a "true child according to a common faith (πίστιν)" (1:4). This signaled for the audience Paul's inclination to define fellowship primarily in terms of "faith" instead of ethnicity or socio-economic class. Even here Paul describes believers as "those who love (φιλοῦντας) us"—those who have experienced the "love-for-human-beings (φιλανθρωπία) of God our savior" (3:4). Such people have been redeemed "from all lawlessness" (2:14) and no longer live "in (ἐν) evil and envy" (3:3) but "in (ἐν) the faith." Greetings are given to this specific group.[55]

Finally, as Paul began the letter wishing the audience "grace (χάρις) and peace from God the Father and Christ Jesus our savior" (1:4), so now he concludes it with a final blessing: "Grace (χάρις) be with all of you." He wishes "grace" upon those who have been saved already by the appearing of the "grace (χάρις) of God" (2:11), which is described later as "the kindness and the love-for-human-beings of God our savior" (3:4). By this "grace" (χάριτι) the "elect of God" (1:1a) have been "made righteous" and "heirs according to the hope of eternal life" (3:7). Like the first blessing, this final blessing serves not only as a prayer wish for more "grace" and a deeper experience of "the kindness and love-for-human-beings of God our savior" (3:4) but also as an indirect exhortation to be conduits of grace, kindness, and love to one another. Having received the "grace of God" in Jesus Christ, the elder is to "exhort with sound doctrine and reprove" (1:9b); the "older women" are to "make sensible the younger women" (2:3–4); Titus is to be a "model of commendable works" (3:7); and all believers are to "learn to engage in commendable works" (3:14) "so that nothing is lacking" (3:13) for any of them.

The apostle's wish is for "grace" to be "with all (πάντων) of you" for whom "all things (πάντα) are clean" (1:15); "with all" who have been redeemed from "all (πάσης) lawlessness" and cleansed to be a "special

55. See Knight, *Pastoral Epistles*, 359–60.

people" (2:14); "with all" who show "all (πᾶσαν) gentleness to all (πάντας) human beings" (3:2). Thus Paul's blessing is not only a prayer wish for more "grace . . . from God the Father and Christ Jesus our savior" (1:4) but also an indirect exhortation for the audience to love "all" the "elect of God" (1:1a)—having experienced the "love for human beings of God our savior" (3:4)—namely by exhorting and reproving one another to commendable works according to the hope of eternal life.

SUMMARY OF CHAPTER SIX

1. The fourth microchiasm (3:4–15) consists of four elements and progresses the theme "Exhort and Reprove to Commendable Works according to the Hope of Eternal Life."

2. In the opening element (3:4–8a) of the chiasm Paul commands Titus to "insist" on "these things," which includes the "faithful word" (3:8a) and the appropriate corresponding conduct. By doing so Paul continues to exercise his apostleship through Titus. Recognizing the influence of the opponents who are "teaching what is not necessary" (1:11) and who are "unqualified for all good work" (1:16), Titus is to "insist" on "these things" so that the audience "may be intent to engage in commendable works" (3:8a). Recognizing Paul's apostolic authority, the Cretan community must stop "paying attention to Jewish myths and regulations of human beings who turn away from the truth" (1:14) and pursue instead "commendable works," having been made "righteous by his grace" and having "become heirs according to the hope of eternal life" (3:7).

3. In the B (3:8b–9a) and B' (3:9b–13) elements the apostle draws a clear distinction between what are "commendable and useful to human beings" (3:8b) and what are "useless and worthless" (3:9b). Not only are Titus and the Cretan community to avoid the latter but they are also to reprove a "heretical human being" and dismiss him ultimately "after a first and second warning" (3:10–11). Instead of getting entangled in "foolish controversies" the audience are to minister to those in need, "so that nothing is lacking for them" (3:13).

4. In the A' element (3:14–15) Paul reiterates the importance of "com-
    mendable works" (3:14) in view of "the kindness and the love-for-
    human-beings of God our savior [that have] appeared" (3:4). The
    specification of "commendable works" as "urgent needs" progresses
    the audience's understanding of their calling as a "special people"
    who are to be "zealous for commendable works" (2:14). The audi-
    ence, in turn, are "to engage in commendable works" according to
    the exhortation and reproof that the apostle gives through Titus. In
    this way, they serve as a rich means of grace to one another.

7

Summary and Conclusion

*Exhort and Reprove to Commendable Works according to
the Hope of Eternal Life*

Having given summary conclusions for each of the four micro-chiastic units in the preceding chapters, in this concluding chapter I summarize how the letter to Titus, with the aid of the dynamic progression of its chiastic structures, exhorts and reproves the implied audience to commendable works according to the hope of eternal life.

The A unit (1:1–4), which introduces the letter, reveals not only how Paul has experienced God's grace and empowerment as a "slave of God and apostle of Jesus Christ" (1:1a), but also how he responds to this love and calling by exercising his apostleship in writing the letter. In doing so, he exemplifies how "recognition of the truth" must be "according to godliness" (1:1b). The central elements of this first chiastic unit communicate to the audience Paul's "hope of eternal life" (1:2a), about which the "elect of God" (1:1a) may be confident because it was promised by "God, who cannot lie" (1:2b). This vivid description of God challenges the audience to reject their cultural norms, which not only accepted deceit but to some extent encouraged it. At the climactic conclusion of the chiasm Paul highlights his unique status in the history of salvation as the proclaimer of the "word" (1:3) who has now given authority to Titus (1:4a). The introductory prayer-wish for "grace and peace from God the Father and Christ Jesus our savior" (1:4b) prepares the audience to receive further grace by listening carefully to what "Jesus Christ" will communicate through his faithful apostle.

The B unit (1:5–13a) expresses to the audience Paul's purpose for leaving Titus in Crete—"to appoint, according to city, elders, as I directed you" (1:5). The extensive list of requirements for the "blameless" elder (1:6–8) advances the audience's understanding of the meaning of "godliness" (1:1b). The elder must be a "lover-of-strangers, a lover-of-goodness, sensible, righteous, devout, self-controlled" (1:8). This standard of being "blameless" is what all the "elect of God" (1:1a) should aspire towards. The central elements of the second chiastic unit highlight the particular quality of "holding fast to the faithful word that is according to the teaching, so that he might be able both to exhort with sound doctrine and reprove those who oppose" (1:9a-b). The center of the chiasm establishes an explicit connection between the "faithful word," which is God's "word" in the apostle's "proclamation" (1:3) concerning the "hope of eternal life" (1:2a), and the call to exhort and reprove. The conclusion of the chiasm identifies for the audience the identity of "those who oppose" as "rebels, empty-talkers and deceivers, especially those of the circumcision" (1:10). Because they are "upsetting whole households" by "teaching what is not necessary," and because they embody the Cretan stereotype of being "liars" (1:12) in contrast to "God, who cannot lie" (1:2b), the audience recognize that "it is necessary to silence" these opponents (1:11). The closing element leaves the audience with the lasting impression that these false teachers not only represent the antithesis of the "blameless" elder but also stand in opposition to Paul and to Titus, a "true child according to a common faith" (1:4).

According to the B' unit (1:13b—3:3) the audience are to "live sensibly (σωφρόνως) and righteously (δικαίως) and godly in the present age" (2:12), pursuing the "blameless" standard expected of the elder who, according to the B unit (1:5–13a), must be "sensible (σώφρονα) [and] righteous (δίκαιον)" (1:8). By doing so the audience demonstrate their allegiance to Paul and Titus versus "those who oppose" (1:9b). The adjective "sensible" (σώφρονας) in 2:2 and 2:5, its verbal cognates (σωφρονίζωσιν, σωφρονεῖν) in 2:4 and 2:6, and its adverbial cognate (σωφρόνως) in 2:12 of the B' unit not only recall the quality of being "sensible" (σώφρονα) in 1:8 of the B unit but also highlight the universality of this quality for all believers in view of their common "hope" (2:13a)—"the appearing of the glory of our great God and savior Jesus Christ" (2:13b).

Specifically the "younger women" are to be "lovers-of-husbands (φιλάνδρους), lovers-of-children (φιλοτέκνους), sensible (σώφρονας), chaste, homemakers (οἰκουργούς), good (ἀγαθάς), submitting to their own husbands (ἀνδράσιν)" (2:4–5) in the B' unit like the elder who must be the "husband (ἀνήρ) of one wife, having faithful children (τέκνα)," and who is described as a "steward" (οἰκονόμον) and called to be "a lover-of-strangers (φιλόξενον) [and] a lover-of-goodness (φιλάγαθον)" (1:6–8) in the B unit. Similarly, cognizant of the apostle's condemnation of "those who oppose" (ἀντιλέγοντας) in 1:9b of the B unit, Christian "slaves" are to be careful "to be pleasing, not those who oppose (ἀντιλέγοντας)" (2:9), "so that they might adorn the doctrine (διδασκαλίαν) of God our savior" (2:10b).

"Sensible" living is possible only when Titus, according to the B' unit, "reproves" (ἔλεγχε, 1:13b), "speaks what is consistent with sound doctrine (ὑγιαινούσῃ διδασκαλίᾳ)" (2:1), and "exhorts" (παρακάλει, 2:6, 15a) like the elder who must, according to the B unit, "exhort with sound doctrine (παρακαλεῖν τῇ διδασκαλίᾳ τῇ ὑγιαινούσῃ) and reprove (ἐλέγχειν) those who oppose" (1:9b). By presenting himself "as a model of commendable works, incorruption in doctrine (διδασκαλίᾳ), seriousness, and sound word (λόγον) that is beyond reproach, so that the opponent might be put to shame, having (ἔχων) nothing bad to say about us" (2:7–8), Titus demonstrates for the Cretan community what is expected of the elder who must be "blameless," "having (ἔχων) faithful children" and "holding fast to the faithful word (λόγου) that is according to the teaching (διδαχήν)" (1:6–9a).

In the B' unit (1:13b—3:3) Paul condemns "human beings who turn away from the truth" (1:14) as "defiled and unfaithful" (1:14–15), "vile and disobedient and unqualified for every good work" (1:16). The audience are therefore presented with a clear contrast between the "clean" and the "defiled and unfaithful" through the explicit comparison between the elder and false teachers. Being equipped with this knowledge, they are to pursue godliness according to the exhortation and reproof communicated by Titus (2:1–10a), the model elder, who speaks "what is consistent with sound doctrine" (2:1). This doctrine, according to the center of the chiasm, is the "sound word" (2:8) concerning the "grace of God [that] has appeared" (2:11) and the second "appearing of the glory of our great God and savior Jesus Christ" (2:13b). By "holding fast to the faithful word that is according to the teaching" (1:9a), the audience are empowered to "live sensibly and righteously and godly in the present age" by "denying ungodliness and worldly desires" and "awaiting the blessed hope" (2:12–13a). Their pursuit of "godliness" (1:1a) demonstrates their "recognition of the truth" that Jesus Christ "gave himself on behalf of us, so that he might redeem us from all lawlessness and cleanse for himself a special people, zealous for commendable works" (2:14). At the conclusion of the chiasm Paul reminds the audience "to be ready for all good work" (3:1) in contrast to the false teachers who are "unqualified for all good work" (1:16). The statement that "we too were *once* . . . disobedient" (3:3) reiterates for the audience their break from those who are still "vile and disobedient" (1:16). Recognizing further the disparity between the "clean" and the "defiled" (1:15), the audience are to reject the "rebels, empty-talkers and deceivers" (1:1) who are "teaching what is not necessary" (1:11) and follow instead the exhortation and reproof of Titus.

In the A unit (1:1–4) that introduces the overall chiastic structure of the letter Paul states that he is a "slave of God and apostle of Jesus Christ . . . on the basis of the hope of eternal life" (1:1a-b). This "hope" is shared between Paul who "was considered faithful (ἐπιστεύθην) according to the command of God our savior" with the "proclamation" (1:3) concerning the "hope of eternal life" and Titus, a "true child according to a common faith (πίστιν)" (1:4). In the concluding A' unit Paul declares that the audience also, who together with Paul and Titus are "those who have faith (πεπιστευκότες) in God" (3:8a), have "become heirs according to the hope of eternal life (ἐλπίδα ζωῆς αἰωνίου)" (3:7). In addition, the prayer wish for "grace and peace from God the Father and Christ Jesus our savior" (1:4), which is addressed directly to Titus in the A unit, progresses to the prayer wish that "grace be with all of you," which is addressed directly to Titus and the Cretan community in the A' unit. Paul's repeated use of the pronoun "our" (1:3, 4; 2:8, 10, 12, 13, 14; 3:3, 4, 5, 6, 15) alerts his audience to their fellowship with the apostle and Titus "according to a common faith" (1:4). In contrast, "human beings who turn away from the truth" (1:14) and are "defiled and unfaithful" (1:15) have no fellowship with the apostle and therefore are not included in Paul's use of "our."

At the beginning of the A' unit Paul reiterates the paradoxical nature of God's salvation: although Paul, Titus, and the Cretan community were not saved "from works that we did in righteousness" (3:5), "those who have faith in God" (3:8a)—having been "made righteous by his grace"—are to "be intent to engage in commendable works" (3:8a). At the center of the fourth and final chiastic unit the audience are commanded to "avoid" the things that are "useless and worthless" and to "dismiss a heretical human being after a first and second warning" (3:8b–11). Instead, they are to focus on the things that are "commendable and useful" (3:8b) "so that nothing is lacking" for those in need (3:13). The end of the chiasm and of the entire letter both exhorts the audience again "to engage in commendable works" and reproves them from being "unfruitful" (3:14). The concluding blessing functions not only as a prayer wish but also as an indirect exhortation for "those who love us in the faith" to extend "grace" to one another through continual exhortation and reproof on the basis of the hope of eternal life (3:15).

In summary, the chiastic structure of the letter to Titus begins by highlighting for the audience the "hope of eternal life" that belongs to the "elect of God," which includes the letter's audience. "Recognition of the truth"—a complete embrace of this "hope"—must be "according to godliness," that is, it must be accompanied by a life that reflects the character of "God, who cannot lie" and an awareness of the significant progress that has taken place in salvation history. At the center of the chiasm, the audience hear that the elder must "exhort with sound doctrine and reprove those who oppose" (1:9b) and that Titus must "speak and exhort" (2:15a) "what is consistent with sound doctrine" (2:1). According to "the doctrine of God our savior" (2:10b), "the grace of God has appeared . . . training us, so that by denying ungodliness and worldly desires we might live sensibly and righteously and godly in the present age, awaiting the blessed hope, the appearing of the glory of our great God and savior Jesus Christ" (2:11–13b). Chiastically developing the theme of pursuing "godliness" "on the basis of the hope of eternal life" (1:1b–2a), the letter concludes on a climactic note that those who "have become heirs according to the hope of eternal life" (3:7) must "engage in commendable works" (3:8a, 14), given the "grace" they have received "from God the Father and Christ Jesus our savior."

In conclusion, listening carefully to the dynamic progression of the intricate chiastic patterns of the letter to Titus challenges and empowers its audience to exhort and reprove one another to "live sensibly and righteously and godly in the present age" in view of the "grace of God [that] has appeared" (2:11) and in view of the second "appearing of the glory of our great God and savior Jesus Christ" (2:13b). In short, the letter itself serves as the challenge and empowerment to exhort and reprove one another on the basis of the hope of eternal life.

Bibliography

Agnew, Francis H. "The Origin of the NT Apostle-Concept: A Review of Research." *JBL* 105 (1986) 75–96.

Balch, David L., and Carolyn Osiek. *Families in the New Testament World: Households and House Churches*. Louisville: Westminster, 1997.

Barr, James. *Biblical Words for Time*. SBT 33. London: SCM, 1969.

Barrett, Charles Kingsley. *The Pastoral Epistles*. New Clarendon Bible, New Testament. Oxford: Clarendon, 1963.

———. *The Signs of an Apostle*. Philadelphia: Fortress, 1972.

———. "Titus." In *Neotestamentica et Semitica: Studies in Honor of Matthew Black*, edited by E. Earle Ellis and Max Wilcox, 1–14. Edinburgh: T. & T. Clark, 1969.

Bassler, Jouette M. *1 Timothy, 2 Timothy, Titus*. Nashville: Abingdon, 1996.

Bauckham, Richard. "Pseudo-Apostolic Letters." *JBL* 107 (1988) 469–94.

Blomberg, Craig L. "The Structure of 2 Corinthians 1–7." *CTR* 4 (1989) 3–20.

Botha, Pieter J. J. "The Verbal Art of the Pauline Letters: Rhetoric, Performance, and Presence." In *Rhetoric and the New Testament: Essays from the 1992 Heidelberg Conference*, edited by Stanley E. Porter and Thomas H. Olbricht, 409–28. JSNTSup 90. Sheffield: Sheffield Academic, 1993.

Bowman, Robert M., Jr. "Jesus Christ, God Manifest: Titus 2:13 Revisited." *JETS* 51 (2008) 733–52.

Breck, John. "Biblical Chiasmus: Exploring Structure for Meaning." *BTB* 17 (1986) 70–74.

Brouwer, Wayne. *The Literary Development of John 13–17: A Chiastic Reading*. SBLDS 182. Atlanta: Society of Biblical Literature, 2000.

Brox, Norbert. "Zu den persönlichen Notizen der Pastoralbrief." *BZ* 13 (1969) 76–94.

Bruce, F. F. *The Letters of Paul: An Expanded Paraphrase*. Grand Rapids: Eerdmans, 1965.

Bruggen, Jakob van. *Die geschichtliche Einordnung der Pastoralbriefe*. Wuppertal: Brockhaus, 1981.

Bühner, Jan-Adolf. "avpo,stoloj." In *EDNT* 1:142–46.

Campbell, R. Alastair. *The Elders: Seniority within Earliest Christianity*. Studies of the New Testament and Its World. London: T. & T. Clark, 1994.

———. "Identifying the Faithful Sayings in the Pastoral Epistles." *JSNT* 54 (1994) 73–86.

Carter, Warren, and John Paul Heil. *Matthew's Parables: Audience-Oriented Perspectives*. CBQMS 30. Washington: Catholic Biblical Association, 1998.

Classen, Carl Joachim. "A Rhetorical Reading of the Epistle to Titus." In *Rhetorical Analysis of Scripture*, edited by Stanley E. Porter and Thomas H. Olbricht, 427–44. Sheffield: Sheffield Academic Press, 1997.

Collins, Raymond F. *1 & 2 Timothy and Titus: A Commentary*. NTL. Louisville: Westminster John Knox, 2002.

Craffert, Pieter F. "The Pauline Household Communities: Their Nature as Social Entities." *Neot* 32 (1998) 309–41.

Dewey, Joanna. "Mark as Aural Narrative: Structures as Clues to Understanding." *Sewanee Theological Review* 36 (1992) 45–56.

D'Angelo, Mary R. "Eusebeia: Roman Imperial Family Values and the Sexual Politics of 4 Maccabees and the Pastorals." *Biblical Interpretation* 11 (2003) 139–65.

Dibelius, Martin, and Hans Conzelmann. *A Commentary on the Pastoral Epistles.* Philadelphia: Fortress, 1972.

Donelson, Lewis R. "The Structure of Ethical Argument in the Pastorals." *BTB* 18 (1988) 108–13.

Dover, Kenneth J. *Greek Popular Morality in the Time of Plato and Aristotle.* Berkeley: University of California Press, 1974.

Dunn, James D. G. *Baptism in the Holy Spirit.* London: SCM, 1970.

———. *The Living Word.* London: SCM, 1987.

Easton, Burton Scott. *The Pastoral Epistles: Introduction, Translation, Commentary and Word Studies.* New York: Scribner's Sons, 1947.

Edwards, J. Christopher. "Reading the Ransom Logion in 1 Tim 2,6 and Titus 2,14 with Isa 42,6–7; 49,6–8." *Bib* 90 (2009) 264–66.

Fee, Gordon D. *1 and 2 Timothy, Titus.* NIBC 13. Peabody, MA: Hendrickson, 1988.

———. *God's Empowering Presence: The Holy Spirit in the Letters of Paul.* Peabody, MA: Hendrickson, 1994.

Fellows, Richard G. "Was Titus Timothy?" *JSNT* 81 (2001) 33–58.

Foerster, Werner. "Eusebeia in den Pastoralbriefen." *NTS* 5 (1959) 213–18.

Glancy, Jennifer A. *Slavery in Early Christianity.* Minneapolis: Fortress, 2006.

Glasscock, Ed. "The Husband of One Wife Requirement in 1 Timothy 3:2." *BSac* 140 (1983) 244–58.

Gray, Patrick. "The Liar Paradox and the Letter to Titus." *CBQ* 69 (2007) 302–14.

Guthrie, Donald. *The Pastoral Epistles: An Introduction and Commentary.* TynNTC 14. Grand Rapids: Eerdmans, 1990.

Hanson, Anthony T. *Studies in the Pastoral Epistles.* London: SPCK, 1968.

Harris, Bruce F. "Syneidesis (Conscience) in the Pauline Writings." *WUNT* 24 (1962) 173–86.

Harris, Murray J. *Jesus as God: The New Testament Use of Theos in Reference to Jesus.* Grand Rapids: Eerdmans, 1992.

———. "Titus 2:13 and the Deity of Christ." In *Pauline Studies: Essays Presented to F. F. Bruce*, edited by Donald A. Hagner and Murray J. Harris, 262–77. Grand Rapids: Eerdmans, 1980.

Harrison, James R. *Paul's Language of Grace in Its Graeco-Roman Context.* WUNT 172. Tübingen: Mohr Siebeck, 2003.

Harvey, A. E. "Elders." *JTS* 25 (1974) 318–32.

Hasler, Victor. *Die Briefe an Timotheus und Titus.* Zürich: Theologischer Verlag, 1978.

Heil, John Paul. "The Chiastic Structure and Meaning of Paul's Letter to Philemon." *Bib* 82 (2001) 178–206.

———. *Colossians: Encouragement to Walk in All Wisdom as Holy Ones in Christ.* Society of Biblical Literature 4. Atlanta: Society of Biblical Literature, 2010.

———. *Empowerment to Walk in Love for the Unity of All in Christ.* Society of Biblical Literature 13. Atlanta: Society of Biblical Literature, 2007.

————. *The Meal Scenes in Luke-Acts: An Audience-Oriented Approach.* SBLMS 52. Atlanta: Society of Biblical Literature, 1999.

————. *Philippians: Let Us Rejoice in Being Conformed to Christ.* Society of Biblical Literature 3. Atlanta: Society of Biblical Literature, 2010.

————. *The Transfiguration of Jesus: Narrative Meaning and Function of Mark 9:2–8, Matt 17:1–8 and Luke 9:28–36.* AnBib 144. Rome: Editrice Pontificio Istituto Biblico, 2000.

Jeremias, Joachim. "Chiasmus in den Paulusbnefen." ZNW 49 (1958) 145–56.

Jewett, Robert. *Paul's Anthropological Terms: A Study of Their Use in Conflict Settings.* AGAJU. Leiden: Brill, 1971.

Johnson, Luke Timothy. *Letters to Paul's Delegates: 1 Timothy, 2 Timothy, Titus.* New Testament in Context. Valley Forge, NJ: Trinity, 1996.

Kelly, John N. D. *A Commentary on the Pastoral Epistles.* HNTC. Peabody, MA: Hendrickson, 1987.

Kidd, Reggie M. "Titus as Apologia: Grace for Liars, Beasts, and Bellies." HBT 21 (1999) 185–209.

Knight, George W. *The Pastoral Epistles: A Commentary on the Greek Text.* NIGTC. Grand Rapids: Eerdmans, 1992.

————. *The Faithful Sayings in the Pastoral Letters.* Kampen: J H Kok, 1968.

Ladd, George E. *The Blessed Hope.* Grand Rapids: Eerdmans, 1956.

Lieu, Judith. "'Grace to You and Peace': The Apostolic Greeting." BJLR 68 (1985) 161–78.

Lightman, Marjorie, and William Zeisel. "Univira: An Example of Continuity and Change in Roman Society." CH 46 (1977) 19–32.

Linton, Gregory. "House Church Meetings in the New Testament Era." *Stone-Campbell Journal* 8 (2005) 229–44.

Longenecker, Bruce W. *Rhetoric at the Boundaries: The Art and Theology of the New Testament Chain-Link Transitions.* Waco: Baylor University Press, 2005.

Lund, Nils Wilhelm. *Chiasmus in the New Testament: A Study in the Form and Function of Chiastic Structures.* Chapel Hill: University of North Carolina Press, 1942.

MacDonald, Margaret Y. "Slavery, Sexuality and House Churches: A Reassessment of Colossians 3.18–4.1 in Light of New Research on the Roman Family." NTS 53 (2007) 94–113.

Malherbe, Abraham J. "'Christ Jesus Came into the World to Save Sinners': Soteriology in the Pastoral Epistles." In *Salvation in the New Testament*, edited by Jan G. van der Watt, 331–58. NovTSup 121. Leiden: Brill, 2005.

Man, Ronald E. "The Value of Chiasm for New Testament Interpretation." BSac 141 (1984) 146–57.

Marshall, I. Howard. "The Christology of Luke-Acts and the Pastoral Epistles." In *Crossing Boundaries: Essays in Biblical Interpretation in Honor of Michael D. Goulder*, edited by S. E. Porter, P. Joyce, et al., 167–82. Leiden: Brill, 1994.

————. *A Critical and Exegetical Commentary on the Pastoral Epistles.* ICC. Edinburgh: T. & T. Clark, 1999.

Matera, Frank J. *New Testament Theology: Exploring Diversity and Unity.* Louisville: Westminster John Knox, 2007.

Merkle, Benjamin L. *The Elder and Overseer: One Office in the Early Church.* Studies in Biblical Literature 57. New York: Peter Lang, 2003.

Miller, James D. *The Pastoral Letters as Composite Documents.* SNTSMS 93. Cambridge: Cambridge University Press, 1997.

Mounce, William D. *Pastoral Epistles.* WBC 46. Nashville: Thomas Nelson, 2000.

Nielsen, Charles M. "Scripture in the Pastoral Epistles." *Perspectives in Religious Studies* 7 (1980) 4–23.

Nolland, John. "Grace as Power." *NovT* 28 (1986) 26–31.

Ollrog, Wolf-Henning. *Paulus und seine Mitarbeiter: Untersuchungen zu Theorie und Praxis der paulinischen Mission*. WMANT 50. Neukirchen-Vluyn: Neukirchener Verlag, 1979.

Quinn, Jerome D. *The Letter to Titus: A New Translation with Notes and Commentary and an Introduction to Titus, I and II Timothy, The Pastoral Epistles*. AB 35. New York: Doubleday, 1990.

Rengstorf, Karl H. *Apostleship*. Oxford: Basil Blackwell, 1952.

Reumann, John H. P. "'Stewards of God': Pre-Christian Religious Application of Oikonomos in Greek." *JBL* 77 (1958) 339–49.

Richards, E. Randolph. *Paul and First-Century Letter Writing: Secretaries, Composition and Collection*. Downers Grove, IL: InterVarsity, 2004.

Saucy, Robert L. "Husband of One Wife." *BSac* 131 (1974) 229–40.

Schlarb, Egbert. *Die gesunde Lehre: Häresie und Wahrheit im Spiegel der Pastoralbriefe*. Marburg: Elwert, 1990.

Schrage, Wolfgang. *The Ethics of the New Testament*. Philadelphia: Fortress, 1988.

Schwarz, Roland. *Bürgerliches Christentum im Neuen Testament: Eine Studie zu Ethik, Amt und Recht in den Pastoralbriefen*. ÖBS 4. Österreichisches Katholisches Bibelwerk, 1983.

Sell, Jesse. *The Knowledge of the Truth—Two Doctrines*. Frankfurt: Lang, 1982.

Shiner, Whitney. *Proclaiming the Gospel: First Century Performance of Mark*. Harrisburg, PA: Trinity, 2003.

Smith, Kevin and Arthur Song. "Some Christological Implications in Titus 2:13." *Neot* 40 (2006) 284–94.

Spicq, Ceslas. *Saint Paul: Les Épîtres Pastorals*. 2 vols. EBib. Paris: Gabalda, 1969.

———. "Le Vocabulaire de l'esclavage dans le Nouveau Testament." *RB* 85 (1978) 201–26.

———. "oivkono,moj." In *TLNT* 2:568–75.

Standhartinger, Angela. "Eusebeia in den Pastoralbriefen: ein Beitrag zum Einfluss römischen Denkens auf das entstehende Christentum." *NovT* 48 (2006) 51–82.

Stelzenberger, Johannes. *Syneidesis im Neuen Testament*. Paderborn: Schöningh, 1961.

Stepień, Jan. "Syneidesis: la conscience dans l'anthropologie de Saint-Paul." *RHPR* 60 (1980) 1–20.

Stirewalt, Martin Luther. *Paul, the Letter Writer*. Grand Rapids: Eerdmans, 2003.

Strauch, Alexander. *Biblical Eldership: An Urgent Call to Restore Biblical Church Leadership*. Littleton, CO: Lewis & Roth, 1995.

Thiselton, Anthony. "The Logical Role of the Liar Paradox in Titus 1:12, 13: A Dissent from the Commentaries in the Light of Philosophical and Logical Analysis." *Source of Biblical Interpretation* 2 (1994) 207–23.

Thomson, Ian H. *Chiasmus in the Pauline Letters*. JSNTSup 111. Sheffield: Sheffield Academic Press, 1995.

Towner, Philip H. *The Goal of Our Instruction: The Structure of Theology and Ethics in the Pastoral Epistles*. JSNTSup 34. Sheffield: JSOT, 1989.

———. *The Letters to Timothy and Titus*. NIGTC. Grand Rapids: Eerdmans, 2006.

———. "Pauline Theology or Pauline Tradition in the Pastoral Epistles: The Question of Method." *TynBul* 46 (1995) 287–314.

Van Neste, Ray. *Cohesion and Structure in the Pastoral Epistles*. JSNTSup 280. London: T. & T. Clark, 2004.

Wainwright, Geoffrey. "Praying for Kings: The Place of Human Rulers in the Divine Plan of Salvation." *Ex Auditu 2* (1986) 117–27.

Wallace, Daniel B. *The Basics of New Testament Syntax*. Grand Rapids: Zondervan, 2000.

Welch, John W. "Criteria for Identifying and Evaluating the Presence of Chiasmus." In *Chiasmus Bibliography*, edited by John W. Welch and Daniel B. McKinlay, 211–49. Hildesheim: Gerstenberg, 1981.

Wendland, Ernst R. "'Let No One Disregard You!' (Titus 2:15): Church Discipline and the Construction of Discourse in a Personal, 'Pastoral' Epistle." In *Discourse Analysis and the New Testament*, edited by S. E. Porter and J. T. Reed, 334–51. JSNTSup 170. Sheffield: Sheffield Academic Press, 1999.

Wieland, George M. "Roman Crete and the Letter to Titus." *NTS* 55 (2009) 338–54.

White, L. Michael. "Social Authority in the House Church Setting and Ephesians 4:1–16." *ResQ* 29 (1987) 209–28.

Winter, Bruce W. *Roman Wives, Roman Widows: The Appearance of New Women and the Pauline Communities*. Grand Rapids: Eerdmans, 2003.

———. *Seek the Welfare of the City: Christians as Benefactors and Citizens*. Grand Rapids: Eerdmans, 1994.

Witherington, Ben. *Letters and Homilies for Hellenized Christians: A Socio-Rhetorical Commentary on Titus, 1–2 Timothy, and 1–3 John*. Downers Grove, IL: InterVarsity Academic, 2006.

Wolter, Michael. *Die Pastoralbriefe als Paulustradition*. FRLANT 146. Göttingen: Vandenhoeck und Ruprecht, 1988.

Wright, N. T. "Paul's Gospel and Caesar's Empire." In *Paul and Politics: Ekklesia, Israel, Imperium, Interpretation; Essays in Honor of Krister Stendahl*, edited by Richard A. Horsley, 160–83. Harrisburg, PA: Trinity, 2000.

Young, Frances M. "On Episkopos, and Presbyteros." *JTS* 45 (1994) 142–48.

23848658R00083

Made in the USA
Middletown, DE
05 September 2015